When Richard Bewes asked me ___ to possible endorsement, he fel___ 'Just dip in here and there; that ___ for you. If you are a 'dipper in', whatever you ___ I did: my first 'dip' was page one, and the first sentence and I was hooked. I couldn't stop reading till I reached the very end! I can't think of anyone who has Richard Bewes' capacity for the telling detail; who is his equal in the helpful development of an idea and in the apt illustration drawn both from wide reading and a wide experience of life and Christian ministry. Many a time I was not only moved, but moved to tears. as Richard brought me to the feet of Jesus, wrote of His centrality, all-sufficiency, supremacy, glory and coming again. I find myself renewed in appreciation and understanding of the Cross, more deeply convinced and in love with the Bible, more penitent and regretful of my past and present, more determined about prayer, more knowledgeable, more equipped – and more aware of Jesus. A truly great and effective piece of writing!

Alec Motyer
Well-known Bible expositor and commentary writer, Poynton, England

In this little volume Richard Bewes has produced another treasure – a masterpiece of practical Christianity, really – for the Lord's people everywhere. Here is a book you can give to a seasoned believer, a new Christian, or someone just pondering the claims of faith. A special gift from one of the most gracious ministers of the gospel I have known.

Timothy George
Founding dean, Beeson Divinity School of Samford University
Birmingham, Alabama

Richard Bewes is a long-distance runner and a true soldier of the Lord. This is a book that – with its balance of the Spiritual and Practical – is urgently needed to help us avoid the serious mistakes made in Christian work and ministry. I would urge all to read it and obtain extra copies for others. We can learn so much from the passing on of this valuable legacy.

George Verwer
Founder of Operation Mobilisation, Kent, England

This book is a great resource for the church, full of biblical insight and practical wisdom. It will be of great use for anyone involved in upfront ministry, doing one-to-one work, or simply working as part of a team. I will certainly be commending it to all my students.

Richard Trist
Dean of the Anglican Institute, Ridley Melbourne Mission and Ministry College, Melbourne, Australia

At the centre of this book is the conviction that Christ will use every believer in His service – that Christian workers are not just church employees but all who serve in any and every capacity. From the practical details of serving in the life of the church to the challenge of living an authentic Christian life, blameless without hypocrisy, pure in heart, Richard's desire is to equip us for increasingly effective service. Written with Richard's typical wit and clarity this book is thoroughly enjoyable, edifying and personally challenging.

Fiona Ashton
Widow of Vicar of St Andrew the Great, Mark Ashton, Cambridge, England

This is a timely book, full of distilled spiritual wisdom and practical advice from one whose long experience in Christian leadership and ministry has had a profound impact on countless lives worldwide. Richard Bewes' passion to help equip us for effective service, leadership and teamwork is highly infectious - and all to be undergirded by the power of prayer – 'The Secret Weapon'.

John Perry
Former Bishop of Chelmsford and Southampton, England

EQUIPPED TO SERVE

RICHARD BEWES

CHRISTIAN
FOCUS

Richard Bewes is the author of several beloved books of faith, including *Talking About Prayer, 150 Pocket Thoughts*, and *The Goodnight Book*. Bewes was the rector of All Souls Church in the centre of London from 1983 until his retirement in 2004. In 2005 he was awarded an OBE for his services to the Church of England.

© Richard Bewes 2013
paperback ISBN 978-1-78191-286-7
epub ISBN 978-1-78191-305-5
Mobi ISBN 978-1-78191-306-2

10 9 8 7 6 5 4 3 2 1

Published in 2013
by
Christian Focus Publications Ltd.,
Geanies House, Fearn, Ross-shire,
IV20 1TW, Scotland, Great Britain
www.christianfocus.com

Cover design by Daniel van Straaten

Printed by
Bell and Bain, Glasgow

CONTENTS

Dedication

My warmest thanks to Dr Mike Reeves for writing the Foreword to this book, and to those at Christian Focus Publications for their production work and their editing – augmented in the U.S.A. by Linda and Kath Nikitin, of Michigan. My wife Pam and I dedicate these pages to all in our respective families – in Surrey, Hampshire, London and Rhode Island, U.S.A. – in thanksgiving for their wonderful support of us, in the months following our first wedding anniversary, shortly before publication.

Foreword

It was ten minutes to go before the main Sunday morning service at All Souls Church, and a group of us were in the vestry, waiting for Richard Bewes. Having just got off an overnight flight from Africa, he had been hotfooting it from the airport to make the service and see the church family. Then he entered the room.

He was clearly very tired from his trip, and jet-lagged. But I'll never forget what happened next: instead of collapsing in a chair with a sigh, round the room he went, person to person, looking us each in the eye with obvious care and concern, asking how we were. There was nothing forced or dutiful about it; it was simply Richard, revealing his kind and pastoral heart.

That heart is clear to see in this book – a book I've long hoped he would write – as he shares some of the wisdom he has learned in his many years of ministry. It is a very practical book, helpfully covering everything from public speaking to private prayer, but with Richard it never drops into pragmatism. Through it all, the heart of a shepherd is modelled, explained and gently pressed upon us.

My prayer, then, is that this book will pass on the torch, equipping you with practical wisdom and instilling in you the passions and the character of a Christ-like evangelist, leader, servant and pastor.

Michael Reeves

Introduction:

Ready for Anything!

We'll be kind and not name the local branch of a national Christian youth organisation in Britain, whose annual Birthday Service I was once asked to address. It was a Sunday afternoon when I drove up to the hall. The chairman met me and showed me into the meeting hall.

There were chairs set out, and at the front a table on which rested a flower arrangement, and a couple of song books at the ready for us. We took our places behind the table. Finally, the chairman cleared his throat and rose to speak.

'Welcome to this, our annual Birthday Service this afternoon. Let us commence our time by singing together from the book number forty. Four-O. *Bind us Together Lord, bind us together, with cords that cannot be broken.*' The pianist struck up.

I was finding it difficult to find my voice at this point. Apart from the chairman, the pianist and myself, there was only one other person in the hall; a young man in his late teens, sitting at the front of several rows of carefully-laid-out chairs. Were we going to make a go of it? Apparently so:

There is only one Lord
There is only one King.
There is only one Body
And that is why we sing –
Bind us together, Lord…..

The format stayed unchanged throughout; our two selves in the 'platform party', the pianist at the side and the single individual before us.

'And now for the announcements!' came the wooden declaration from the front.

Whatever my actions were when it came to my turn has been thankfully blotted out of my memory. The episode, however, was but a single lesson among many over the course of several decades: *In Christian service, we have to be ready for anything!*

I think of an African friend of mine, a fine Christian worker in central Africa. His name is Babaka. Frustrated by the poor content of the broadcasts from his local radio station, he finally found the courage to make contact and offer his services.

'If you give me just one hour a day, I can fill it for you for nothing!'

'Very well', came the response. 'We'll let you have five o'clock every morning.'

Babaka rearranged his life for a daily broadcast of Bible preaching, rising at four each morning. Weeks of broadcasting went by. Babaka began to wonder, *Is anyone listening out there at five in the morning?*

He put it to the test. 'Hey, if there's anyone listening to me on these mornings, I'd like to meet you one day; have tea and some fellowship. Shall we agree on a date?' A venue and day were given out. You know what happened? One hundred and twenty thousand people turned up! The lesson came strong and clear: *In Christian work, we have to be ready for anything!*

Are you in Christian work? 'Oh,' people say, 'Not me. I'm not a missionary or Sunday School teacher, let alone a church minister.'

No? But do you get to serve with others in the church…. in your student or youth group? You do the coffee? You visit and phone people? You pray for your workmates? You get to the prayer gathering? *Anyone who gets to a prayer meeting is a Christian worker!* The pages that follow may help in being 'Prepared for every good work' (2 Tim. 2:21, NKJV) . But remember….

In Christian work, we have to be ready for anything!

Part One:

You're Up at the Front

Where do you feel weak today? When you borrow from God the strength, courage and joy you don't have, people can't help but notice. Just make sure they know where it came from!

JONI EARECKSON TADA
Pearls of Great Price (Zondervan)

1

Telling Your Story

'I'm Alan – do you remember me? You led me to faith in Jesus ten years ago just outside Cambridge.'

I had never forgotten that evening. I had been a student then, and one November night the college Christian group had sent three of us out to a nearby locality in what was called a 'Team of Witness'. Roy Leverson – then studying for church ordination – was leader. 'Just tell your stories of beginning with Christ,' he told his two teammates, David Watson and myself. For me it was the start of a long friendship with David Watson, who was to become an outstanding church pastor and evangelist of the future.

But neither David (who had only just come to belief himself) nor I had ever done anything like this before. 'Just tell your story!' explained Roy. *'Three things!* You say something about life before you came to Christ, then when and how you came to the great Decision and finally the difference that knowing Christ has made!'

I began to think it through. Why, it had happened for me only five years earlier, during a week of summer activities run by the Scripture Union for about a hundred of us teenagers in the English county of Dorset. The attraction for me was the tennis coaching – under a Wimbledon player by the name of Douglas Argyle.

A personal decision

It being a Christian event, prayers were held every morning and evening – and I could cope with that.... until the day when one of the leaders came up to me. 'Come for a walk, Richard!' I sensed danger, but could only comply. Sure enough, my mentor eventually worked round to his question: Had I ever accepted Christ into my life?

I lied. 'Oh yes, I've done that!'

– 'That's great! When was that?'

I thought rapidly. 'About two years ago.' It sounded like a reasonably safe enough time to have elapsed.

– 'Wonderful! And how did that come about?'

I took a deep breath, and invented a little story, making it up as I went along. Having been brought up in a missionary family, I knew the language well enough! Honour seemed satisfied; the man was happy enough – and I'd got him off my back.

But it was during those very days that my personal decision was indeed made, as I listened to a man called Mr Nash, speaking at the evening prayers. At one point in his talk, he began to refer to the Cross of Jesus Christ, and opened his Bible at Isaiah 53, verse 6:

> All we like sheep have gone astray; we have turned every one to his own way, and the LORD hath laid on Him the iniquity of us all. (KJV)

Mr Nash closed his Bible and placed it on his left hand. 'Now,' he said, 'we can read the sentence in this way. Suppose this left hand represents you and me, in all our sinfulness and rebellion against God. And suppose that this black object represents the weight and penalty of our unforgiven sins, crushing us down.

'And suppose that my *right* hand here represents Christ, in all His purity and goodness.... and then suppose' – and Mr Nash looked up at the electric light above him – 'that the *light* there represents God in all His love, and desire to forgive us.... NOW we can read the sentence like this:

'All we like sheep have gone astray;' the speaker was looking at his left hand, 'we have turned every one to his own way, and the LORD' – Mr Nash looked up – 'hath laid on *Him* the iniquity of us all.' By then the Bible on the left hand had swiftly been transferred to the right hand. The left hand was now empty.

Mr Nash looked at us all. 'Now where are your sins?' he smiled. I got the point immediately. The responsibility of the world's sins had now been taken by Christ – who had died for me. Eternal forgiveness could be mine. I also learnt that Christ, now raised from the dead, could be my unseen Companion, giving me power for daily living.... if that was what I wanted. *And I did want it.* All that remained for me actually to do was to thank the Lord for coming to me in love – and then personally to accept Christ as Saviour and Lord.

Tonight I'm going to do exactly what that man says, I silently resolved. Nothing was going to stop me. I waited until the end-of-day banter and laughs were all over. Then in bed, I sat up and prayed, admitting that I was sorry for having kept Christ out of my life until now. I thanked Him for dying for *my* sins, and opened the door of my will for Him to be Lord of my life from then on.

* * *

Now at college, so much had happened since that night five years earlier, and I resolved to try to get some of my story

across. I made some notes on a piece of paper, rehearsed –
and prayed. Then we set off for the village hall.

It was at the close of the meeting that the young man in
Britain's Royal Air Force approached me.

'I'd like to know more.'

It was Alan. I had never before consciously led someone
to personal faith. We sometimes call it *The Way of Salvation*.

The bad news, the good news

There's the *Bad News*, I explained to Alan: that rebellion
against our Creator describes every one of us, and that
we are not fit for God's presence in this life or the life to
come. There was the *Good News*, I went on to say – that
God in Jesus came to us in love through His Son's death
on the Cross for our sins – so offering us free forgiveness
and friendship with Him for ever. And there's *The Way In*,
I challenged – as men and women repent of their sins and
personally accept Jesus Christ as Saviour and Lord, and go
on, empowered by His Spirit, to live effectively for Him.

Something of this must stumblingly have got across to
Alan as we chatted. Then for a while he stayed silent, head
down, and finally lifted his gaze. 'I've accepted Jesus into
my life,' he declared.

Later that night, I could hardly sleep for wonder. *I could
die right now*, I thought. *For the first time ever, I've publicly told
my little story and astoundingly it's been used to tip someone into
Christ's kingdom.*

Yet there are plenty of people who, across the years, have
lastingly touched the lives of many for God, without ever
consciously leading someone through 'the Way of Salvation'.
There need be no guilt trip about this, for there is no neat and
tightly practised formula by which someone must come to
faith. As Augustine put it sixteen centuries ago, *'One loving
spirit sets another on fire.'* At a Christian 'outreach' party once

in London, I was speaking with a man of another religion. 'So what brings you here?' I asked.

He pointed at a young man across the room. 'I'm only here because of *him*. The way he lives and speaks has got through to me, and I've come to find out what it is that makes him different from me.'

Let's also establish that there are believers – like the late Ruth Graham, wife of the famous evangelist – whose personal 'story' is that from childhood they were brought up to know and follow Christ; they never knew anything else. So a precise 'before and after' pattern has not always been typical for them. Yet their story is of Christ at the centre of their lives!

Everybody has a story

What then is *your* story? Everybody has a story, and Christian believers do well to think through, analyse, and even prepare and *rehearse* their stories – for that occasion when, with a friend, we can naturally 'give the reason for the hope that is within us' (1 Pet. 3:15, KJV).

Or indeed for that occasion when we are asked to get up in public at the front! This need not be too frightening. First, your story can be naturally drawn out of you in interview-style.

TIP: Work out beforehand whether there is some Scripture sentence that has particularly meant a lot to you and to which you can draw attention at some point. You need not preach a sermon about it, for this is not the point at which you must put out a strong 'appeal'; that can be left for whoever gives a further address in the programme. This is simply your 'story'.

Alternatively, you may be asked to stand up front and give a three-minute address. *TIP*: Make some notes on a piece of paper. But not on a large attention-deflecting sheet! It can be done well enough with a small, business-like ring pad, measuring perhaps five inches by four.

And the Roy Leverson instruction is *right*, time and again. **Before**.... **What Happened**.... **the Difference** it has made. Others have done it ahead of you! Read the whole of chapter 26 in the book of Acts, and you will see this pattern in the personal account given by the apostle Paul as he stood before King Agrippa.

It's our story of Christ

We can also see from Paul's words that his story was a story of CHRIST in his life. That is the whole point. If Christ is in your story, and if there are those prayerfully supporting you as you give it, you can expect that heaven will use it!

I shall never forget an outreach evening service at the English parish church of St Peter's, Harold Wood, Romford. As leader of the congregation at that time, I had invited the church treasurer to tell his story as part of the service. He was a short man, with spectacles, called Peter Haigh. His could have been described as a non-dramatic, simple account of entering into Christian discipleship. He had never given it before; indeed, he had never spoken as a Christian in public before.

During the service my attention was riveted by the presence, near one of the church pillars, of a visitor – the deputy headmaster of a nearby comprehensive school. I had met him before, outside the life of the church, and he was formidable. Agnostic, intellectual, cynical – and with a rasping voice that could cut down all opposition – he had no problems with discipline from his pupils. Evidently, a colleague had brought him along. As one of his pupils who was present said to me afterwards, 'When I saw him there, I thought, "It looks like him but it can't be." And then I realised it *was*!'

Two days later, I heard that the deputy head had become a Christian that very night. It seemed unbelievable. Finally, I caught up with him.

'It wasn't so much your sermon,' he explained. 'It was that man whom you got up at the front to tell his story. And while he was speaking, I could *feel* the whole congregation pulling for him, wanting him to do well. I had never experienced such a thing in all my life. That's what turned me over. So I've accepted Jesus Christ and become a Christian.' We watched my new friend's life changing; the whole church became aware of what seemed like a miracle.

Think about it, then. When you are asked to tell your story in public, *you won't be alone.* You are likely to have a bunch of supporters all around you, who have been praying ahead for that moment when you totter to the front and begin to speak of Christ in your life! And you can believe that, by His unseen Spirit, His pledged presence will be right beside you.

2

Reading the Bible in Public

But is this a necessary topic? I'm afraid so. I have heard the British actor David Suchet declare that he has been up and down churches everywhere…. and that the dull and listless public reading of the Scriptures is generally a disgrace to the power of the Bible.

Not that we are without some happy moments! Fred Hurding, a much-loved senior member of a church in north-east London, opened his Bible as he faced the congregation. 'The reading this morning is taken from the letter to the Ethiopians,' he began.

Bewilderment followed…. but we loved Fred for it, knowing that his life as an east Londoner had earlier revolved entirely around dog racing; that he was a comparative newcomer to church life – and to the Bible.

'Good morning, church!' boomed the voice of big Sherman Whitefield, as he opened the lectern Bible before the congregation of All Souls, in central London. Sherman was from America's Deep South.

Silence.

'Ah say-ed, "GOOD MORNING, CHURCH!"'

A cheerful response greeted Sherman.

'Well, folks, we're gonna look right now at the book of Is-ayah, and chapter si-ixty-si-ix, and a-a-all the way thru' to verse twenny-fo-ur. Here we go! "This is what the Lord say-es" – *and I like this bi-it!'*.... And so the reading progressed.

On another occasion, in the account of Christ's Transfiguration we heard one reader declare that 'a cloud came down and *ONveloped* them.'

Happy incidents of this kind become a valued part of a church's memory bank.

But realise that it is the Scriptures that have built the church today into the biggest and fastest-growing family of belief that the world has ever seen. How great, then, is the importance of the simple activity of public Bible reading!

'The music was wonderful today'.... 'That was a great talk!'.... 'I loved the worship!' Comments like these can flow out at the close of many church meetings – but hardly ever do I hear gratitude expressed for a Scripture reading.

Carelessness with the Bible
One reason is that in a number of churches and in Christian 'celebrations' scant attention is being given to the Bible at all. Much is given over to the music.... and cascades of singing. It is to be hoped that one day Scripture reading will come into its own again – just as happened to Judaism in the fifth century B.C. At that time the seventy long years of Jewish exile, imposed by the Babylonians, had ended, and the days of national reconstruction were under way. The temple had been restored in Jerusalem, the laws had been reinstated under Ezra, the scribe, and the city wall re-built under Nehemiah, the governor.

Next came the grass-roots desire for a new national constitution:

All the people assembled as one man in the square before the Water Gate. They told Ezra the scribe to bring out the Book of the Law of Moses, which the Lord had commanded for Israel. (Neh. 8:1)

If the people had coined a mission statement or national slogan for their newly emerging identity, it might have been, *IN GOD WE TRUST*. Instinctively – despite all the years of being cut off from the taproot of their national life – they sensed that their destinies were bound up in those five foundational books of Moses.

Those chapters 8 and 9 of Nehemiah are as crucial to every nation struggling for an identity as anything you could parallel in history. Today major political groupings in a score of countries have their seasonal conferences year after year. Without exception they struggle for the Big Idea that can inspire and unite society.

It would have been 444 B.C. when the returned Jews expressed a holy discontent with a merely well-organised infrastructure. 'Roads, laws and secure walls are all very well,' they were saying, 'but wasn't there a *Book* once?' Before long, everyone was saying it. 'The Book, the Book – we must have it back! Where's Ezra?'

Bible reading – and tears

So Ezra, the scribe, stands up on a specially constructed wooden platform before the entire population, and reads – from daybreak till noon – from the Book. How did the public reading of the Scriptures affect the people? Why, in weeping, in great joy, and in deep repentance (Neh. 8:9, 12, 17; 9:1-3).

Have you ever seen such a thing happening with the public reading of the Bible? It has been known in gatherings of the great East African Revival; men and women would even drop down in the conviction of their sins; then would

be raised in joy with the realisation that their sins were forgiven. I saw it when ministering in Romania, following the
Ceausescu revolution and the collapse of communism, as
the Bible once again was coming into its own. The hunger
was intense, with tears and joy mingling.

Church leaders! **Nothing that God has given us in His
Word can be anything other than powerful.** What attention, then, are we giving to the public reading of Scripture?
In the West, particularly, I have worshipped in many gospel
fellowships in which no one present appeared to be following in the Bible when the Scripture reading was announced.
The church may even be sufficiently well off to have Bibles
provided at every seat, *but the Bibles stay closed.*

The issue of PowerPoint

'Oh' – it is explained – 'we now have the passage displayed
on a screen at the front, by *PowerPoint.*' It often happens
that the same procedure is followed for the preaching.
I have frequently observed that even the preacher will not
be carrying a Bible, relying instead on the *PowerPoint* display, perhaps on a private monitor screen.

PowerPoint certainly has its use in the giving of announcements from the front. It can also perhaps help a congregation unite in the words of a song or hymn, and even
improve the singing as eyes are lifted. Against that are the
disadvantages, first, of not seeing at a glance the entire
sung item (or indeed the service order as a whole?) and secondly, of worshippers being unable to take back home – and
familiarise themselves with – the words of inspiring songs
printed on a giveaway service sheet.

And with the Bible? Which is better: to display
a chosen passage in isolation on a screen, or to encourage
worshippers (including those unfamiliar with the Bible)

to get used to *handling the text for themselves, and find their own way around....* indeed, to learn the art of checking whether the preaching itself is fully in agreement with the surrounding passages? True, some can always turn up a Bible passage on their iPhone, but there is something romantic – even exciting – about the rustling of pages in a true Bible church!

Let all this be the background to that occasion when you find yourself called upon to read from the Scriptures in a public gathering. Don't denigrate the opportunity by thinking, *Of course, I'm hardly in the class of the preacher, or worship leader; I'm just a useful, fill-in bit while people can sit for a moment and have a break.* Think back, rather, to those Jews, as Ezra mounted the rostrum and began to read. Be like the Levites present – in the dramatic assistance they were giving to what was a wonderful occasion!

> They read from the Book of the Law of God, making it clear and giving the meaning so that the people could understand what was being read. (Neh. 8:8)

That is exactly the task. **We are not simply pronouncing words when we stand at the front.** Well ahead of time, the Scripture passage should be in front of us as we prepare the chosen reading, and pray, 'Open my eyes, that I may see wonderful things in your law' (Ps. 119:18). *Unhurried preliminary prayer is vital to the task.* What is this passage all about? Why is it here in the Bible? What is its main point? In order to help the listeners to understand what is being read, I need to ask myself which words – as I read them – could do with a slight emphasis, a mental underlining, a raised or lowered inflexion?

And yet I am not to be there at the front in order to draw attention to myself! Others should not be thinking, 'What a great reader,' but rather 'My goodness, that passage was speaking to *me*!'

Use of the Voice

The voice must be naturally your own. No extra 'holy' solemnity needs to be injected into the reading. If, some day, you switch on your radio at random and a church service is being featured, *it is all too often immediately recognizable as such.* The prayers, the readings, the sermon – and the final blessing come across in what can only be described as a 'churchy' art form. Do normal people speak with such affectation? Did Jesus, when telling His parables?

We are to keep the speaking voice natural, and yet with an underlying awareness that – without straining – **we need to project.** Many are the occasions when those present have to struggle to hear the words of a reader, and particularly when the voice drops at the close of every sentence. True, there may be a microphone before you, but be not deceived! It is only there to impart a slight 'lift' to the voice; it simply cannot do the job for you.

TIP: On getting to the front, you will be, perhaps, within six or nine inches of the microphone. *Ignore the microphone completely and simply let go* – with the aim of projecting your voice to the very back row of the people in front of you. That way you are likely to be heard.

Categories to avoid

Across the years I have recognised various unfortunate 'categories' of reader. Be warned! They can come under various apt titles or descriptions. An obvious one I have tended to name after an early English king who unfortunately became known as **Ethelred the Unready.** Such a reader turns up; has clearly not thought through how the passage is to be announced and where it is to be found, let alone worked out a one-sentence description of what it is about. The sentences have not been thought through, names are mispronounced – the reading is an utter non-event.

By contrast we have sometimes been subjected to **The Thespian.** Here a well-intentioned reader is so intent on 'acting' the passage with ham-fisted phoney 'accents' imparted to the dialogue sections as to make it truly cringeworthy. Of course, a planned and invited dramatic reading is quite a different matter. The problem with the amateur thespian, however, is that all attention is likely to fasten on the individual concerned, rather than on what God is saying through His Word. *Public Scripture reading can be truly supernatural in power – without it ever becoming unnatural in delivery.*

Have you sometimes heard **The Dullard** give the reading? It is delivered in a flat monotone throughout; sometimes gabbled through with no emphases or inflexions whatever; it could have been a recitation of shares on the stock market. Any drama or high point in the passage is simply ironed out.

Then there is what may be called **The Queen's Speech.** The voice is immaculate; all is beautifully spoken and with perfect diction. Many present will comment favourably. 'What a wonderful reader!' But somehow the reading lacked 'Soul'. Was it a communication from heaven and a life of prayer, or a performance from the local dramatic society?

Further painful categories could be added – but we can leave it there!

It is no bad thing to give yourself some practise sessions. Try Luke 15:11-24 as an obvious 'story', and then, by contrast, Ephesians 2:1-10, and again – in the Old Testament – 1 Kings 18: 20-39.

Treat it as an honour to get the feel and flow of God's Word, and then to express its richness and power as you read it before a gathering. For centuries the Bible has been described in the British Coronation service as *The most precious thing that this world affords*. We are to treat it like that!

3

Leading in Public Prayer

Leading a public gathering in prayer! The approaches can vary across cultures and personalities. Who is to say that the phraseology of a Billy Graham team member was out of place when – after a day of hectic office work in the city – he inadvertently closed his prayer at a public meeting with 'So we thank you, Lord, for your presence with us today. Yours sincerely, John Dillon.'

Naturally, informal intimacy has often characterised the prayers of Christians *on a private, individual level*, often with verbs and nouns in a loose jumble. No problem! The great hymn writer John Newton commented, 'Five words, a few broken sentences from a broken and contrite heart, are more desirable than to pray for hours without spiritual feeling.' And intimacy in prayer stems ultimately from Jesus' teaching to His friends that they had direct access to One they could call their heavenly 'Father' – a title that is not used in any other major religion. Fears, hopes, joys and disappointments they learnt to bring to Him. No matter if they had no polished phrases with which to approach Him. He was, after all, their heavenly Father.

I was speaking of this privilege in Christian prayer with a man of another belief-system. Then I asked, 'And how do you pray?'

'*We recite,*' he answered.

I was able to explain that it's better news than that! A way of immediate access has been opened, I said – right into the very throne room of God Almighty – by the sacrificial death of Jesus for the sins that would otherwise shut me out of God's presence. Because Christ has died for my sins, has been raised from death and has now ascended to the right hand of God, He has the authority – both as God and as perfect Man – to conduct me, as one of His recognised followers, directly to the divine Throne.

'I can come', I added, 'with my own words as someone adopted into God's family, at any time of day or night!'

My companion sat down beside me. 'You know, I could become a Christian,' was his wistful response.

It's not that there is no place for prayers from a *book* in our daily walk with God. We can benefit from books containing the richness of prayers from earlier Christians. More importantly, there are prayers in the Bible itself – from prophets, apostles and lovers of the Lord – that we can make our own. Prayer is a lifelong education!

But what can be learnt about the prayers we may be invited to lead on behalf of others in a public gathering? Such opportunities will often be in the context of the leading of the *intercessions*, the general 'asking' prayers.

What Public Prayers are not

First, these are not your 'private' prayers, spoken out loud. At this specific moment in the fellowship, you are the 'spokesperson' on behalf of everyone present – with the aim of expressing, as far as possible, what we are *all* wanting to say to God. So it is not '*I pray that…*' but rather,

'*WE pray that....*' And when people tell you at the end of the meeting, 'I liked the prayers,' they mean that **they felt able to identify personally with what you were saying from the front;** your prayers had become THEIR prayers.

That is, provided they could hear you! Microphones at the front are useful, but we still need to speak out our prayers in more than a conversational voice – loud and clear for those in the back row to take in and confirm with their firm 'Amen'.

Second, these are not opportunities to issue sidelong rebukes, preach mini-sermons or to make political points, (though I do wonder why, in the prayers of many of our UK churches, our own monarch scarcely ever receives a mention). *Our prayers are to be directed heavenwards.* And care needs to be taken, if PowerPoint is used, that no extravagant visual illustration be allowed to divert attention from the Lord Himself. Worshippers have probably been deflected in their prayers if inwardly they are murmuring, '*What a beautiful picture!*'

Third, these should not be prayers designed for exclusive use within the inner core of the fellowship. All too often, public prayers feature the use of 'insider' language – in terms of first names only, unfamiliar Christian shorthand jargon and baffling, acronyms that give the impression of an exclusive, cosy 'in-group': '*Today in prayer we continue to remember John, doing tent-making in Djibouti with O.M. We also pray for Alastair, now going out with Y-WAM....*'

The uninitiated thinks, 'John who? And what's this about his making *tents*? Is O.M. some pal of his? And who, I wonder, is the girl Wai Wam, whom Alastair is going out with; are they getting engaged?'

Fourthly, our prayers are to be thoroughly Christian. To whom are we praying? We need to shun sloppy terminology, and recognise – from the start – that the Lord may be addressed by a variety of titles.... *Almighty and everlasting God.... God and Father of our Lord Jesus Christ.... O Lord our God.... Sovereign Lord.... Lord Jesus.... Heavenly Father....* At times our prayers will be addressed directly to Jesus – again, with the remembrance of the variety of His various titles and names. **And let us watch the ending.** It is only right to end with a phrase that indicates the basis on which we can come to God at all; for example, 'Through Jesus Christ our Lord. Amen'.... 'We pray this in Jesus Christ's name, Amen' .... 'We pray this for the sake of Christ our Lord, Amen.' To end in this way has the advantage, first, of giving a congregation a signal, by which all can join in unitedly with a confident 'Amen'. More importantly, it is an education to everyone – including those from other beliefs and no belief – that *it is only by the Name of Christ, our once-crucified and now ascended Mediator, that our prayers have any access to the holy presence of God.*

A useful checklist

In my own experience, the leading of a crowd of others in prayer – just to try to get it right – is pretty much as hard as preaching! First, then, ***prepare yourself*** spiritually for this task. Ask for the help of the Holy Spirit as you get ready to lead the people of God to His throne. Is there any greater or graver privilege?

Second, ***school yourself.*** What you will be doing is not the same as the initial public confession of sin, the 'praise and worship' part of the meeting (which is likely to be the responsibility of someone else). Your responsibility is to lead all present in both thanksgiving and the outreach of the gathering in heartfelt intercession. Say to yourself, as you prayerfully prepare, *By these prayers, our church is going to touch the world!*

Third, it may be valuable to **script yourself.** It is not 'unspiritual' to do this. It must be remembered that others will want to 'own' the words and phrases that we use. The *rambly* prayers can be kept for the occasions when we are surrounded by our own trusted friends.

Part of the value of scripting ourselves lies in a determination that we are not going to slip into the boring, well-worn phrases that have done the rounds of certain church circles and become hallowed into a kind of acceptable churchy *art-form.* 'Let's just bow our heads' is an obvious evangelical cliché that I rid myself of many years ago.

Fourthly, **time yourself!** You will be amazed. The unspoken fear of many is that we may misuse – or underuse – this opportunity that God has placed before us. Consequently, *many publicly offered prayers are frequently filled with interminable and unnecessary matter.*

Notice my word *'prayers'* – for there is no reason why we should not divide our prayer into separated segments, each with its own separate theme or request. *REASON:* When heads are down and eyes closed, many people's concentration dies at about twenty-five seconds! Twenty-five seconds for a single prayer may feel absurdly short, *but then it is the spirit and depth of the prayer that matters, far more than the verbiage and length.*

Fifthly, **Confine yourself** to carefully *selected* aspects, persons or countries within the work of God. More than once I have heard a prayer that begins, 'We pray for all people....

everywhere.' Naturally, we wish to touch the world, but we cannot cover everybody! If there is a theme running through the meeting, allow it to colour the prayers. Often the study of a single sentence of Scripture can shape the prayers that will follow.

Are we done? Not really. But we can finish, once again, with a few cautions!

Some cautionary profiles

'The Noticeboard': We have heard them often enough; prayers that are basically *announcements* about the precise time and location of coming events – and even useful travel directions! 'Announcements' are sometimes made, albeit prayerfully disguised, that are pointedly designed to tell those listening what to do or even how good we all are! The hypocrisy of the religious leader in Jesus' parable of Luke 18:9-14 is a warning to all whose prayers contain any other interests than those of heaven itself.

The Tour Operator: These are the prayers that take God's people everywhere – from national elections in one country to earthquakes in another; to current news items, missionary updates, international tensions, inter-church conferences…. and, within a few minutes, heavy breathing has taken over a gathering that is only waiting for relief. *Then comes the final killer:* 'And now, coming closer to home, we pray on further for….'

'Our Parish is our World': This is entirely on the opposite tack; the theme of the prayers being entirely local in their emphasis. Whereas many years ago the evangelist John Wesley could declare, 'The world is my parish!', the belief in some circles would be, 'Our parish is our world!' Their prayers revolve entirely around internal issues:

births, deaths and marriages, arrivals and departures, local happenings and minor calamities. Any thought of global events outside, and of a world church faced with challenges and persecution, is absent. The deity addressed seems to be no bigger than a local village chieftain.

The Prayer of the 'Just' Person: These are the public prayers that, once you analyse them, contain no specifics at all. They are sometimes couched in the cliché-ridden 'blessed' language of earlier times; alternatively in a recognizable mid-Atlantic accent and with mid-Atlantic terminology – with the word 'just' used as a convenient punctuation mark, as in 'We just want to give thanks....'

The Punctuation Mark: So what about *punctuation-mark* prayers? These are the prayers that no public gathering can easily adjust to, in that they are entirely on-the-spot and haphazard in their utterance, sometimes in the mistaken belief that only so does the Holy Spirit inspire our praying. Because these prayers have had no constructive thought given to them, the names *Father.... Lord.... Jesus.... God....* are used interchangeably throughout and very frequently – and as little more than useful commas. This is no honouring way in which to address the Persons of the Godhead.

But ultimately, it is the Heart that drives any prayer! Years ago, when Princess Diana died, a woman on our church council led the Sunday prayers in church – and was shaking with sobbing grief. It was so fitting that she had been asked to lead. For as John Bunyan once observed, 'In prayer it is better to have a heart without words, than words without heart.'

4

Planning the Meeting

My friend William was doing business in a country that has been hostile to Christianity for many decades when – on a particular Sunday – he ventured into a household where a meeting was being discreetly held for about forty people. Singing and prayer took place, and the Scriptures were being read and explained.

Afterwards, William approached a young woman who had been busy at the back, working on a laptop.

'What were you doing during the meeting?' he asked. 'Were you taking notes?'

'No,' came the reply. 'I was busy, admitting hundreds of people into the meeting from all over the country – by Skype!'

There is power released by even the smallest of meetings if Christ is present. When the apostle Paul and his friends first arrived in Europe with their Christ-centred worldview they began with a meeting by the side of a river. Next they were at the home of a businesswoman. Later, their mission was based at the house of a man called Jason (Acts 16:13-15; 17:5-9). Never mind if jailings and riots resulted; such is the life-changing and revolutionary power of the message of Jesus Christ!

Now – in the twenty-first century – we may find ourselves called to lead a meeting ourselves, be it for children, enquirers, students, trainees, senior citizens or for the general church gathering. And the initial planning is vital! **What am I out to achieve, as I take on this piece of leadership?** We can be glad enough when we hear that young people – in a Christian summer event – had 'a great time', but in reality the lasting effectiveness of those happenings will only be known twenty years later. *And you simply cannot pass on a great time to the next generation.* What is the central and key objective?

Christ's parting words to His friends were to go and make disciples of all nations (Matt. 28:18-20). The apostle Paul's aim was one of proclaiming Christ, 'admonishing and teaching everyone with all wisdom, so that we may present everyone perfect in Christ' (Col. 1:28). For ourselves, then, **we shall not be satisfied until those whom we lead emerge as mature followers of the Lord Jesus Christ, established firmly in the membership of His redeemed family.**

A leader of a single study 'table' of enquirers in a *Christianity Explored* programme once told me, 'As we begin a new series of meetings, I usually have about ten assigned to my table. From the start I make a note of their names, to pray for them daily, that over the course of time each of them will emerge as firm disciples of Christ.'

Once the overall aim is established, we can then work at the general *approach* which should govern the leader of any Christian meeting. Tips only!

1. The style: Model the local cornershop!

It matters not whether we find ourselves leading a group of ten people, or a mega church of thousands; the style is always to be one of engaging servanthood and easy access.

When our family lived in central London, we were frequently customers at big, well-stocked superstores, but there was something different about the cornershop at the bottom of our road. There would be recognition, warmth and a welcome as we walked in. Across the counter the proprietor would smile.

'Hullo, good morning! Your son was here ten minutes ago; he's gone on to the library right now!'

What was it? Somehow we were treated not as visiting 'customers' so much as accepted *intimates.*

We learn from Jesus in this respect. Those who swarmed around Him were never looked upon as anonymous nonentities who could swell His meetings.

Our very style of operation, then, is to reflect Christ's. First, it is to be **childlike – without being childish.** No dumbing down! Take an example. In the meeting that you may lead, very probably there will be singing. Of all the belief-systems in the world, Christianity is about the only one that takes singing seriously. Others may chant, recite or meditate, but it is our delight to sing! In choosing songs or hymns, then, one of my tests has been to ask myself, 'Can I imagine a top athlete…. someone from the media…. someone just out of prison, a parliamentarian or congressman…. coming into our meeting and cheerfully singing this chosen item – and not cringing at the words as childishly stupid or just plain "wet"?'

While always recognising the value of informal music, be alerted, then, by Voltaire – that stern critic of established Christianity two hundred and fifty years ago. Of some of the music in his own day, he sarcastically commented, 'If a thing is too silly to be said, it can always be sung!'

Take it further. The style is to be **supernatural without being unnatural.** I remember someone of another religion coming into a Christian meeting for the very first time – originally attracted by the lifestyle of a neighbouring Christian believer. Petrified, on entrance, by fear of some strange, paranormal experience, overwhelming relief soon replaced the terror.

'It suddenly dawned on me,' said my new friend. *'These are just ordinary people!'* The result was new life in Christ – and baptism. The secret simply lay in the dedication and prayers of some very 'ordinary people'.

A third desirable, corner-shop style of leadership can be summarised as **directive without being manipulative**. If you are the leader of a meeting, you are required, indeed, to set the tone and *lead*, yet in a manner that reflects, not so much on yourself – for we are but Christ's under-shepherds – but rather on the 'Chief Shepherd' (1 Pet. 5:2-5). It is as we prayerfully submit our work to the Lord that Christ-honouring attitudes are formed. Ahead of time we can pray, *'As I step over the threshold into that meeting, let me carry something of yourself and your own servanthood in with me.'*

Nothing can be achieved in the meeting without a measure of authority and direction. But manipulation by worldly or psychological pressure – however spiritual-sounding its guise – was never Christ's way. If we can get this right, we will be spared from a malaise that all too often afflicts the Christian church today.

2. The attitude: Beware the 'we-you' syndrome!

I am sorry to say we find this in too many circles; a certain assumed 'aura' that betrays itself in mannerisms, speech and body language. Remember Diotrephes, who got his name into the Bible, simply because he loved to have 'the pre-eminence' (3 John 9, KJV)?

It is the *we-you* syndrome. Too often an inner assumption takes over, that 'we' – up at the front – are something of a race apart; that it falls to us to 'disciple' and direct *'them'* – the mere consumers below. It would never be expressed in this way. But it emerges in the vocabulary used. It comes across even in the way announcements are given:

'Hey, we've got a great programme for you all tonight!'

'Right now, what we want you all to do is turn to your neighbour and say, "I love you"!'

'As you go out, you'll see we've put out a box for your gifts….'

It manifests itself in the way that music and items are planned, with the unspoken thought, *If WE put on such an item at THAT particular point, it will make THEM want to respond in THIS desirable way…..*

OR

…. If I can end my talk with this burst of purple oratory (and with no closing prayer), it may draw out some 'spontaneous' applause….

A little cynical perhaps? Believe me, it is not. We church ministers can see these things in ourselves all too clearly! Diotrephes still lives on. We must see to it, then, that 'we-you' is banished from the mindset of every Christian leader.

Not that the leader is to be hidden. There is an understandable tendency among some leaders – and indeed church ministers – to be so 'one of the people' that they modestly sit back among the meeting's members, or even at the very rear, until their time at the front is due. This is fair enough in a very small group, but in any larger gathering it needs to be visibly obvious just who is appointed to keep an eye upon the proceedings from the front – and who is there to take charge at any given moment of urgency or surprise.

3. The structure: Recognise whose meeting it is!

The obvious antidote to the we-you syndrome in our planning is to ask ourselves how we can please *Christ*, and keep Him and His Word central. This has been the great safeguard of the most effective evangelists in all history. They touched many; yet the attention was never fastened on themselves. The entire direction was towards Christ and the building of His church.

One way of planning the meeting is for the leader to face a series of test questions. Here are a few:

First, whose event is this? It was never ours! Indeed it surely 'belonged' to the existing members before we were ever introduced as leader. Thus, ministers and leaders are wise not to use terms such as '*my* class, *my* youth group, or – as I have even heard – *my* "lot"'!

In point of fact, it should be recognised that the meeting belongs to no one at all, beyond our divine Master. *It is actually He who is summoning us, not we who are inviting Him!* Consequently, I have never felt entirely at ease on those occasions when I have heard well-meaning leaders call out, 'And we welcome Jesus to our meeting; let's give Him a round of applause!' True, Christ is God-Incarnate who humbly came among us as the greatest Friend of all, but it is too humanly earthbound publicly to address the Very God of Very God in terms of Best Pal. This realisation should affect our approach to the whole meeting.

Second, how can the meeting inspire and not exhaust?! One answer is to work hard on the overall *shape*. Brian Mickey, a former BBC radio producer, used to exhort his programme assistants, 'Start bright! Then go brighter still. Next, slow it down and finally go out with a bang!' That was one approach. What will be ours? Avoid the drifting, deliberately casual approach of studied mediocrity, or the by-now familiar (and sometimes exhausting) recipe of an endless chain of 'worship' songs. Will the Bible be opened? Has thought gone into the pace, variety, content and timing? Care in these matters will help to ensure that all stay refreshed, *and will be wanting more by the close.*

Third, will those coming have the confidence to bring their trusted friends next time – and every time – without fear of being ashamed? That is the acid test for every meeting and every church! Do those who come have a fair idea of what to expect, or may there be nerve-racking or embarrassing surprises and innovations that leave the members – and newcomers – thinking, *I wonder whatever may be coming next?* As confidence builds, so growth results.

As I finish this chapter, I am shortly to lead a meeting of about twelve people. But littleness matters little to God. You may be leader of a very small meeting – but see yourself at the foot of a picture painted by Henri Rousseau in 1897. It hangs in the Musée d'Orsay in Paris, and depicts a large and formidable-looking *Madame*, claiming virtually the entire canvas. But at her feet the artist included a small cat, playing with a ball of wool. As you step up to view the painting, it isn't three seconds before your eye is drawn irresistibly to the little cat. In the end, it's the cat that dominates.

From God's viewpoint that could be tiny *you*, pictured along with the apostle Paul and those few women by the river, apparently dwarfed within the canvas of mighty, threatening Europe! But Christ's gaze is invariably fastened on His under-shepherds – from apostles onwards…. right through to the modest 'table-leader' of today.

5

'Unaccustomed as I Am...'

'Can't I just stick to helping with the games and the tennis coaching?' At a Christian summer event, I had been informed by the leader that I was to give a Bible talk to about a hundred young people. I shook at the prospect, never having done this before.

But the man was adamant. 'You'll be fine! You'll be on for twelve minutes, and the subject will be *Christian Service*. See if you can find a nice Bible passage to speak from!'

At least I had been given six weeks' warning – and I used those weeks carefully. I found a passage; I wrote copious notes, thought of some stories, then reduced everything to a single card.... and I would lie in bed, night after night, saying my memorised talk over and over to myself.

The day finally drew near. Having observed the knees of the previous morning's speaker shaking with fright, I resolved that the following day I would take a long, hot bath before prayers began, and when I drippily emerged, I was satisfactorily relaxed and somewhat limp. Finally, I stood up to speak and – holding my Bible before me – parrot-like I disgorged the words that I had learnt by heart. My heart was thumping, but my knees were steady.....

New to public speaking?

When we are new to public speaking, the approach and style of the older and more experienced rub off on us. For myself, I learnt from London's Dick Lucas, whose biblical authority all came off the back foot. I learnt from John Chapman, of Australia, whose brilliant talks were like his tennis playing – all seemingly off the *wrong* foot. There have been Alec Motyer, of Dublin, Sami Dagher, of Beirut, and Ron Dunn, of Texas, whose talks fairly crackled with riveting power. There were the fathomless William Nagenda and the bubbly Festo Kivengere, of the East African revival. And there was always John Stott.... There have been women like Anne Graham Lotz, of North Carolina, or the missionary doctor Helen Roseveare.

There was even my Auntie Carol. For I remember inviting Carol Hunt to speak to our church youth group when I was a young man. Wearing a no-nonsense outfit, she stood at the front, about five feet tall:

'You're probably saying to yourselves right now,
"Who's that old bag standing there at the front?"'

And then.... the minutes passed, and nobody stirred. Auntie Carol, indeed, was in demand all over the country for her speaking.

The fact is, **effectiveness in public speaking is independent of the age factor.** You can be 'young' at sixty – alert, flexible, ever-learning and a lover of people. Conversely, some speakers have reached their ceiling by the age of twenty-five. The reason? Their mindset is set in a groove that does not permit them to listen, adapt or learn from anybody. In such a case, their speaking remains at the same level forever. *They have never been 'hungry' enough.*

Working with two columns

My own early preparation has been the same since I was about twenty. At the top of a large sheet of paper I will write the title of the intended talk, and the Scripture reference on which it will be based. It is also important to write down the intended *aim*. But then I draw a line right down the page, some two thirds of the way across. In the larger left-hand column, I scribble down all that I can discover by way of **content**, as I pray over the Scripture passage and gather any further insights from writers and Bible commentators – but always with the thought, *What is the ONE thing that this passage or text is saying? And how, with the help of God, can I best make this clear for my hearers?*

At the same time I am alert for the little stories, observations, memories or quotes that can act as windows that help the light shine through to the dullest of listeners. Jesus did this, and so can we. It's called *Thrillmanship!* **We are not out there at the front to be reading Bible essays aloud till the end of time.** The illustrations and stories are going to help. These may suddenly pop into my mind, and as fast as they come, I will scribble them down – in the narrower, right-hand column. Just a few of them may eventually marry into the material of the left-hand column as inspiration begins to grow. I may even find an old story from the preacher C.H. Spurgeon…. and then it occurs to me, 'I've got a story just like that; I'll use mine!'

The one vital point

It is not that the *stories* are the main substance. The left-hand column is the vital one. And the thought keeps surfacing that I must make sure that any subsidiary points I learn from this passage must relate firmly to the ONE great point the Bible here is getting across. And if they don't, then I have probably got that one main point wrong.

There have been times when I reckon that at last I have understood the one essential meaning of the passage before me. Then I wander off for a bite of lunch – and, on returning once more to my task, it dawns upon me: *No, you haven't got it at all; start again!*

It is a joy when prayers are answered, and the meaning and message begin to surface and captivate your thinking. Now is the time to start writing. Oh, sure, Peter would have used no notes on the day of Pentecost, when over three thousand people responded. But then Peter was an apostle! It is noteworthy that in all the great arenas of the world visited by the evangelist Billy Graham, every address was typed out, word for word, in front of him. True, many public speakers can reduce the notes to a few lines on the back of an envelope. There are even occasions when we know the address so well, that all notes can be abandoned. **But the advantage of writing out the talk – at least initially – is that we can begin to stretch our vocabulary and rid it of those unnecessary phrases, tiring repetitions and all-too-predictable pieces of jargon and *'Ers'* that litter so much modern speech.** There is nothing 'unspiritual' about having every planned word in front of you, provided you know the talk well enough to 'lift' the words off the page as you speak.

Any notes should never be so big that they flap and deflect attention. Either they can be small enough to be contained within the pages of the speaker's Bible, or cut down to a size that will fit on to a lectern or desktop. The only risk is that of unintentionally sweeping the notes on to the floor. I did this once in the famous 'Round Church' of Cambridge – and watched as they floated down and finally came to rest in between a radiator and an adjoining wall. Presumably they are still there.

Supremely, it is the Bible that is to figure! In *The Sermon* series of fifteen-minute expositions given on the Internet by various international preachers (www.thesermon.co.uk), we remind each other to be **holding the Bible and visibly referring to it.**

These days it has unfortunately become popular to preach from an iPad. To all appearances, the iPad is the authority.

Where do the stories come from?

Back to the right-hand column! The question arises: 'Where do we get these illustrations and stories from?' The best answer is, *Let them come to you from all sides, every day.* And as they come, get them immediately on to small index cards, and categorise them alphabetically under the 'obvious' headings: Prayer, Cross, Life, Service, Cost, Sleep, Money, Death, Persecution, Resurrection, Christmas, Science, Power, Creation, Procrastination, Sin....

Go out to a stationer's to buy a card index system, *and begin it today.*

Or set up your system electronically, in a way that you can access the information immediately. Many are the times when I am asked where I get my stories from, and the answer is that **they come to me.** I do not have to find them! I leave alone books of well-known quotes or illustrations. Better for the integrity of our speaking to make helpful notations from books that we have ourselves read, **and to make an immediate record of some event, story or observation the moment it occurs to us.** Do not delay action even for ten minutes, for by then the illustration will have faded like the morning mist.

I began my illustrations system many years ago – in the belief that a journey of a thousand stories begins with a single card. *Across the years this, at least, has been an effortless activity.*

Does it get easier or harder?

Harder, of course, is the left-hand column! I once asked John Stott, 'Do you find that speaking gets easier or harder as time goes by?' His answer was at first a little depressing: 'Oh, it gets harder!'

But his reply was an indication that his studying was forever on the increase and that, consequently, his standards continually rose. His very simple aim, however, remained the same. As he once described the task of unravelling a Bible passage:

What is its natural meaning? Let the words speak for themselves; we are not to twist them to mean something else.

What is its original meaning? In any given passage, the Bible writer is saying *one* thing, and we need to study and work hard to establish what this is. This one meaning should dominate the entire talk.

What is its general meaning? All Scripture holds together; so we will not find some meaning in a single passage that doesn't accord with the rest of the Bible's teaching.

John Chapman, of Sydney, once told aspiring speakers, 'Go for the easy Bible texts or passages; that way you won't mess them up!'

As I write, the latest Bible talk I gave was some days ago. It was on John 4 – Jesus and the Woman at the Well. The passage is concerned with Living Water, an easy topic to illustrate throughout! The main text that I began with, and then worked around, was verse 10, with Jesus saying *'If you knew the gift of God and who it is that asks you for a drink, you would have asked him, and he would have given you living water.'* I then tried to ensure that the whole talk related to this one theme. These were my points: 1. Learn to see Thirst as Unrest. 2. Learn to see Water as a Person. 3. Learn to see Drinking as Believing.

As for the giving of a talk, where to look, how to use a microphone and the use of one's own unique trademark (the voice) – for these and other practical aspects it could be useful to refer to my *Speaking in Public Effectively* (Christian Focus Publications).

You are speaking to one person

Effective public speaking comes out of a background of prayer, meditation, love, grace – and often suffering. Be expectant as you stand up to speak! Silently ask the Spirit of God to fill you, and say quietly to yourself, *In the next few minutes somebody's life is going to be changed.* Messages glow with life-transforming energy when both speaker and listeners are aware that another Voice has taken over. Then it is that someone exclaims, 'I felt it was just for *me!*' Once on British television, Billy Graham was asked how many 'converts' he hoped to win in his forthcoming London campaign. 'One!' was his reply. 'Just one! If I could win *you* to faith in Jesus Christ, it would have been worth coming.' In the end, that's it. In any talk you and I may ever give, it is actually *one person* whom we are addressing.

Years ago, William Magee, of Dublin, declared that there are three kinds of speaker; the one to whom you *cannot* listen, the one to whom you *can* listen and the one to whom you *must* listen!

Part Two:

Together We Stand

'You cannot create a true community without abdication. In order for a group of people to draw together peacefully, we all have to abdicate some positions. We have to change from going higher to going lower, so that the lower may go higher. As we do this, we become a community of servants.'

FESTO KIVENGERE
African Enterprise
Hope for Uganda and the World (Evangel Publishing House, Nairobi)

6

The Building of a Team

Would we ever have picked *them* as the start of a mighty movement, numbering up to two and a half billion devotees across the world? They included some members of the Israeli fishing industry, a taxman with a shady record and a few other unknowns. Not one of them was recognised in religious circles. At one point in their travels with Jesus their Master, they stopped off at a house in Capernaum.

— 'What were you arguing about on the road?' asked their leader.

Silence. They had been dividing up the incoming kingdom of God among themselves.

— *'I suppose in the New Order you think you'll be Secretary of State.'*

— *'Not me. It's the Presidency I'm after.'*

— *'What have you got against me that I can't be Chancellor?'*

Maybe we could forgive them; it was still early days for the twelve disciples. But then step into the Upper Room, just hours before the arrest and death of Jesus. **It's the most sacred moment of all, the very first occasion of the Lord's Supper.** And then it happened yet again. *'A dispute* *arose among them as to which of them was considered to be greatest'* (Luke 22:24).

Up gets Jesus. Silence again. Off comes the tunic, out comes the basin, on comes the towel. *'Your feet please, John…. your feet, Peter….your feet please, Philip.'* It was only slaves who ever touched the feet; the feet were always kept out of sight. Christ's washing of His team members' feet was symbolic of the world's greatest act of servanthood about to take place the next day; the washing through the shedding of blood not only of his few friends from their sins of a lifetime, but of millions upon millions of future believers of every language and country around six continents.

When the evening was finally over, Mark tells us they sang a hymn and went out. *They were hardly singing at the start.* Suppose Peter had earlier announced, 'Let's sing Number 15, everybody!' Just then they could hardly look into each other's faces. But hearts repeatedly melt at the actions of Jesus.

The proving of servanthood

As with Jesus, servanthood in a team tends to emanate from the leader. But wherever it arises, it is supremely Christ-centred, highly attractive – and contagious in its effect upon whole churches and regions. It takes only days for a company of Christians to detect whether an incoming evangelist, pastor or worker arriving among them is a true servant. *We must learn this well.* Not until we have proved our servanthood can anything of lasting significance be achieved in the things we take on for Jesus Christ.

Undoubtedly there are those who, often through circumstance, are called out as lone pioneers in extending the kingdom of God – frequently in some of the most troubled areas of earth. But, in general, the very idea of 'church' assumes our doing of things *together.*

Start with modest involvement!

Generally team membership is initially learnt and tested by the means of modest involvement. A former colleague of mine, Alex Ross, was to become a pastor and preacher of very high attainment and international renown. But earlier, while still at Bible college, he was assigned to assist in a church that I would eventually lead in north-west London – there to learn something of service in a local setting. Later, I learnt that *the one task Alex was given, Sunday by Sunday, was to carry a box of toys into the infants' group, unload them, stay around to 'help', and eventually repack the box.* And, despite Alex's considerable Bible knowledge, nothing else. Upfront 'Word Ministry'? There was none for him! But he proved to everybody's satisfaction that he was a cheerful and loyal team member. On my eventual appointment as leader to that church, I was urged by Alex's college principal, Dr Gilbert Kirby, 'Make sure Alex Ross comes on to the full-time pastoral team!

John Newton, who – two centuries ago – was transformed from slave trader into one of the church's most godly ministers and hymn writers ever, once declared in a conversation:

> If two angels were to receive at the same moment a commission from God, one to go down and rule earth's grandest empire, the other to go and sweep the streets of its meanest village, it would be a matter of entire indifference to each which service fell to his lot, the post of ruler or the post of scavenger; for the joy of the angels lies only in obedience to God's will, and with equal joy they would lift a Lazarus in his rags to Abraham's bosom or be a chariot of fire to carry an Elijah home. (*John Newton*, by Richard Cecil, Christian Focus)

That is the issue! When team members are convinced of a God-given calling, nothing else matters but ambition for the interests of Christ and His people. All private jockeying for position or public adulation is to be ruthlessly shunned.

The Cross sets the standard

On the eve of the crucifixion, the disciples had been vying for greatness. It is from the Bible that we learn that **true greatness is measured by the Cross of Christ** – where sacrifice and self-giving to the interests and welfare of others were to the fore. It has often been said that the ground is level at the foot of the Cross. The disciples were as yet unable to take this in. Why, with these great crowds they were becoming famous; they were on the threshold of power!

And if this mindset could predominate at the last Supper, I fear it can take over any of us, among today's preachers, music bands or worship leaders. It can invade local church elderships and indeed the Christian press – when readers may be invited to send in their opinions on 'the most influential church leaders of the decade', or 'Preacher of the Year'. Could any individual happily achieve prominence in such a poll, under the gaze of Christ? It is when the Cross loses its place in the centre of the team's vision that pride, competition, jealousy and power-seeking take over. Such self-interest can spread to an entire church when – in relation to neighbouring fellowships – it adopts as its unspoken adage *'We have no need of you'*. The selfless message of the Cross was never advanced by solitary empire-building.

The Team's Leader

Whenever someone is called to look after a team – whether they be youth worker, street pastor co-ordinator, bishop or church leader – a threefold task awaits them in the main. They are to PROTECT, to INSPIRE and to UNITE – with the pure teaching of the inerrant biblical gospel behind all three priorities. The central vision is of God who has come to redeem a rebellious, dying world from eternal judgment by the power of His Son's death and resurrection; who is raising a people worldwide who will live to His praise and glory. Once lose that vision – and all protection, inspiration and unity go out of the window, and we are left with a powerless body in confused disarray, however loud the shouting.

Newly appointed leaders of a Christian group or fellowship need not fear too much about their lack of Bible knowledge. We can but learn! But if they are wise, they will know that *the key question relates to the direction in which they intend to lead the team.*

Where is the direction?

My wife Pam and I have long known the Norfolk Broads in England's East Anglia, and the fine view from its waters of the handsome flintstone tower of St Helen's Church, Ranworth. Imagine a boatload of holidaymakers setting off from the boathouse at Ranworth Broad. They are supposed to be heading towards one of three islands, where a picnic lunch is awaiting them. Inside the boat a disagreement is under way.

– 'Look!' says the leader, 'Island A – right ahead. That's where the picnic is. Pull away!'

– 'No!' cries an oarsman. 'It's Island B – just to the right – where we should be heading. Alter course by a tiny fraction!'

– 'Rubbish!' shouts a third. 'You're all wrong; it's Island C, way off left! Change course by ninety degrees!'

QUESTION: Who is the most dangerous person in the boat? At first we might point to the advocate for Island C, so badly off course is the insisted advice. But no. Nobody in the boat is taken in by such a blatant error. The dangerous directions given are those for Island B. It is so close to Island A – and if the boatload of people head out that way, they will only just miss their correct destination.... *but they will miss it.*

The principle of the angle

It is the principle of the widening of the angle. If a church or fellowship veers only half a degree away from what the New Testament describes as *the word of truth.... the good deposit.... the trustworthy message.... The faith once and for all entrusted to the saints* – then ten years down the line will see that group neatly diverted into a distant backwater of spiritual powerlessness, and they won't even know it.

A Christian leader, then, is wise to establish just where future team members are starting from, before appointments are made – however little they may know! How 'hungry' are they? Where are they *intending* to be, in relation to God and the Trinity, to Jesus Christ, to the centrality of the Cross and the way of salvation; to the Holy Spirit, to prayer – and to the inspiration and inerrancy of the Scriptures?

What makes a credible Christian team?

The apostle Paul, though writing alone in his prison chains, was only too aware of his fellowship with others in the great task of reaching Europe. His words to the Christians at Philippi could be taken as a motto text for any group called into teamwork for Jesus Christ:

> Whatever happens, conduct yourselves in a manner worthy of the gospel of Christ. Then, whether I come and see you or only hear about you in my absence, I will know that you stand firm in one spirit, contending as one man for the faith of the gospel without being frightened in any way by those who oppose you. (Phil. 1:27-28)

In this letter, Paul had already written of Defending the gospel (1:7); of Proclaiming it (1:18); now of Exhibiting it. The work is done *together*. And a team cannot avoid being on exhibition. We are to be seen **standing in unity.** We are to see to it that it is the biblical gospel that holds us together; nothing else. Let there be no mistake; the very first time your chosen team meets for Bible study and prayer, it is likely to be apparent within the hour whether you have unity or not. And if the *team* has unity, the wider membership will also be united. And once that happens there can be no stopping you!

Paul also makes it apparent that his friends were to be seen **standing in adversity.** Inevitably, there will be 'those who oppose you'. Suffering is, remarkably, something that is 'granted' to us by the once-crucified Christ (1:29). To stand by each other, prayerfully and practically, when everything is going *wrong*, is to provide the world with an honouring exhibition.

Further, they were to be recognised as **standing in humility.** 'Do nothing out of *selfish ambition or vain conceit.* Rather in humility value others above yourselves' (Phil. 2:3, emphasis mine). At a meeting in the 1880s, the American evangelist D.L. Moody was invited to introduce fellow preacher Henry Ward Beecher. 'Introduce Beecher?' he exclaimed. 'Not I! Ask me to black his boots and I'll do it gladly.'

There's nothing like the power of a close-knit team for God! I think of an African proverb from my own birthplace in Kenya:

'Sticks in a bundle are unbreakable'.

7

Whatever Happens:
Stay Focused!

'Every one of you is to take the day off and go into London,' declared Tommy Garnett, headmaster of Marlborough School. 'We don't want a single one of you fooling around here. Not when there's a Coronation taking place.'

My tennis-playing brother Michael and I looked at each other. Already we knew. In a matter of days, our team would be playing in 'The Youll Cup' against a score and more of schools from around the country.... *at Wimbledon.*

– 'I need to work on my backhand.'

– 'My second serve could do with a lot of polishing.'

– 'We'll have the place to ourselves. Let's spend the whole day on court.'

Never mind a Coronation. **Wimbledon was beckoning.** And when the tournament was over, we would find ourselves selected to play together in a match against the All England Club itself – facing Britain's Davis Cup captain on the other side of the net. *It had been worth that day of focused preparation.*

The principle applies in every imaginable sphere. Watch the top golfers. Read about Michelangelo's painting of the Sistine Chapel in four breathtaking months, or of Handel's writing of *Messiah* in twenty-three days. Take Marie Curie, the discoverer of radium. When questioned by a reporter as to the focus of her greatest need, she replied in terms of a single gramme of radium.

The Christian, of course, must inevitably live in *two* worlds; in the cities of this earth, to be sure, but with the necessary concerns of family, finances, health and the workplace controlled and energised by a higher focus altogether – upon the City that is above. There will be those who pour scorn upon the Christian believer as 'narrow-minded'. But no; the narrowest people around are those whose focus is limited to mortgages, petrol prices, sexual adventures, retirement plans, the cult of celebrity, and a few kind words in the local paper at the end.

The highest focus enhances all else
The Christian, as a child of eternity, starts way ahead of the rest. The everyday and vital components of daily living – far from being sidelined by the one great call of Christ's supreme call upon our loyalties – are actually enhanced. The historian Arthur Bryant, whose works were devoured by Churchill, wrote:

> The Christian faith has been the greatest continuing germinator of human energy at all levels of which there is any record in the annals and achievements of man. (*The Lion and the Unicorn*, Doubleday p. 348)

The Bible, prayer and the church's witness worldwide are all part of the energising power of Christ's mission across civilisation.

The question of how any team of Christian workers can sharpen and preserve its focal point – its mission statement

– in its own locality, is the subject of the pages before us now. This exercise has had to be learnt, often painfully, from the book of Acts onwards! Our mistakes have been plenty, as men and women of God have struggled together, and sometimes failed, at staying focused on the work in hand, whatever happens.

The art of discerning

True discernment and wisdom have nothing to do with academic, religious or political prominence. History's high roads are littered with brilliant and talented individuals – often adored by millions, yet possessed of a poor judgment. Their legacy is one of blunder after blunder, relationship after relationship, catastrophe upon catastrophe. Governments, schools and churches alike suffer as a result.

By contrast, there are those individuals, less naturally endowed perhaps, who have grasped the main objective of their given task perfectly. One such was Nehemiah, butler to King Artaxerxes of Persia twenty-four centuries ago. Called by God to rebuild not only the walls of his stricken city of Jerusalem but also its very spirit and morale, his was a large team of workers! The pressures were immense. Internal division sometimes threatened. Other claims obtruded on his priorities, but they had to take second place.

Undeflected

As early as chapter 2 of the Book of Nehemiah, there features the diversionists – Sanballat and his crony Tobiah. Their tactics were five-fold: first, *to deride* God's servant (Neh. 4:1-3); second, *to distract him*, with an invitation to dialogue (6:2); thirdly, *to exhaust him*, with repeated invitations (6:4); fourthly, *to intimidate him* with an open letter (6:5-7); and fifthly, *to contain him* by coaxing him to quit and stay shut up indoors (6:10, 11).

Nehemiah's goal was simple in its focused discernment: 'I am carrying on a great project…. Why should the work stop…. ?' (6:3). In today's world of Facebook, the Internet, emails, conferences, novel spiritualities, passing fads – and the antics of atheistic institutions – Christian teamwork can be too easily deflected from its main focused aim.

It is not that our eyes should be closed to outside trends and opportunities. But, in taking note of them, we are wise to ask ourselves, *How likely would our engagement with this innovation cause confusion or division among our members? How far does it tie in with the one great focus of what we are doing?*

The art of directing

'Having been brought up on the lower slopes of Mount Kenya,' I confessed to the Rev. Herbert Cragg, 'I know next to nothing about regular ministry in an English church; I'm going to need regular sessions of training under you!'

I had just been ordained to the Christian ministry. It was my first-ever Monday-morning staff meeting in Beckenham, in the south-east of London. The answer from my new boss surprised me.

– 'No, don't worry too much. We'll have times of prayer and fellowship together. The *Caleb Club* – that's the youth work – you'll soon get into. The same with the children's work. We'll each go visiting. And about the preaching…. well, I'm still a babe myself. Just keep your ears and eyes open. And let's each take Thursdays off.'

That was about it. *I did keep my ears and eyes open – for the full six years I assisted Herbert Cragg.* I would watch him like a hawk when he chaired the Church Council, knowing that one day I would be doing the same. Those years at Beckenham got me going. They were about the greatest blessing of my life.

Isn't that roughly how it worked with Jesus and His disciples? Most days they were walking together.... fellowshipping.... eating.... listening and watching. Thus, in any team's development, while 'training seminars' with outside visiting speakers can occupy a useful place, what chiefly matters is *the internal exercise* of standards and attitudes rubbing off from one to another. We work, pray and study together.... forever watching and absorbing along the way. *It's caught as much as taught.* The only danger lies with team members who fail to watch and listen. The risk is that they will never improve beyond their mid-twenties.

The art of entrusting

This can be hard, in a team setting.... especially if you are the leader. Even more so if you are a perfectionist! I found this with chair-arranging. At theological college I was told, 'You are going to be setting out chairs for the rest of your life.'

Consequently I learnt chair-setting as an art form. I would watch my mum and dad as they arranged chairs for the prayer meeting. My father was the optimist, planning for a bumper turnout. Every space tightly filled; chairs bunched together, with rows as narrow as possible. Then I would see my somewhat pessimistic mother quietly going down the rows, and halving the number of chairs. 'Let's eke them out,' she would quietly murmur. In her view, it would be wonderful if anyone arrived.

Mine too was the way of pessimism. Spacing out the chairs carefully, yet informally, you can create the impression of a full room. Psychologically it is always better to call out 'More chairs, please!' rather than to be left gazing dismally at empty seats.

On arrival as leader of the larger city church of London's All Souls, I had to realise that any expertise I had ever gained in chair-arranging was now redundant! There were now lay assistants on hand, whose job description included chair-arranging, under the direction of appointed leaders.

Chair-arranging, then; the giving of notices, publicity flyers, titles for meetings, hymn-choosing, 'Book of the Month' selection – all this, and a whole deal more, may have to be entrusted, at least in part, to others. But that, truly, is how a team grows.

The art of affirming

Back to tennis. In the years when Australians were the dominant power, both in the Davis Cup and in Grand Slam tournaments, it was noted that one of their strengths was the mutually supportive spirit that pervaded their team. Let but one of them step on court in a Grand Slam quarter-final, and the others would be there in the stands, in force.

A team engaged in Christian service can never be a collection of self-motivated individuals. We are there for each other, making up and covering for each other's weaknesses, glad of each other's strengths.

Ask yourself, when speaking of a fellow team member or a neighbouring church minister: *Do these colleagues know for sure that their reputation in the public sphere is safe in my hands?* And jealousy of others is cured when we take pains to praise them for their superior talent – publicly! A miracle of grace then takes hold as the cold, jealous stab within is replaced by the warm glow of Christ's affirming presence.

The art of defusing

But, of course, differences and strains can arise. If you are a church pastor or leader of a team, criticisms may be levelled against you at times. Indeed, you may sense the need to bring a criticism before your colleague. *TIP:* Avoid using emails or text messages. If you have received an unkindly, critical email, *hold back for at least twenty-four hours – and even then, consider before you think of replying.* The damage caused by hasty emails, so often copied to a host of other recipients, must bring nothing other than grief to the Holy Spirit of God. Face-to-face contact is infinitely preferable.

Care must be given to the attitudes with which tensions are dealt. My brother Michael, from his world of business, once explained to me four contrasting reactions: First, **Cold Dominance:** *Very well, as your leader, I can only tell you, If you find it too hot in the kitchen, you can get out and find something else. We've no room here for lame ducks.* Second: **Cold Submission:** *Well, of course, I'm only just a humble servant caretaker in these parts. I'm only too happy to tender my resignation.* Third: **Warm Dominance:** *Hey, fret not! I'm holding the reins; no worries! – Romans 8:28 and all that! Leave it to me....* Fourth: **Warm submission:** *Listen, I think you've got a point; you could be right. Let me go away and think about it. I'll come back to you.*

Of these four, 'Warm' is the only possible approach – bearing in mind that, while *Warm Dominance* is too over-powering, *Warm Submission* by itself may result in nothing happening at all.

––––––––––

Mutual trust is vital in a team setting. After preaching one morning at our first service in central London, I was stopped in the coffee break by my colleague Paul Blackham. 'Before you preach that sermon again in the second service,' he said, 'you need to know that towards the end you made a mistake.'

I was aghast. 'Tell me what it was,' I replied, 'and if I can get time, I'll rewrite that end bit.'

'No need,' said Paul. 'During the closing blessing I wrote out a new ending for you. Here it is!' And he handed me a piece of paper.

That was trust.... Both ways!

8

Secret Weapon:

The Prayer Meeting

Years ago I was on the committee behind *Amsterdam 2000* – Billy Graham's millennium conference that attracted three times more applicants than the 12,000 international evangelists who could finally be accommodated in the great Europa Hall. Besides the plenary sessions, we planned scores of voluntary seminars. While Dr Paul Blackham's session on 'How to explain the Trinity to an Unbeliever in Five Minutes' attracted the greatest demand of all for the resulting CD, I felt a little sorry for the leader of the completely unattended session entitled 'Financial Prudence'.

Never mind! *Do our pulses race at the thought of a seminar – or book chapter – on Prayer Meetings?....for they should!* The New Testament reminds us that we do not wage war as the world does; 'The weapons we fight with are not the weapons of the world. On the contrary, they have divine power to demolish strongholds'! (2 Cor. 10:4). It was Edward Reynolds, of the seventeenth century, who wrote:

Satan hath three titles given in the Scriptures, setting forth his malignity against the church of God; **a dragon**, to note his malice; **a serpent**, to note his subtlety; and **a lion**, to note his strength. *But none of these can stand against prayer.*

This is not only strategic; it is exciting. My colleague Rico Tice, ministering in central London, was asked by a neighbouring church leader, 'Anything exciting happening at your church?'

– 'Yes,' replied Rico. 'We're reading the Bible and we're praying!'

– 'Oh, well, *yes*,' came the reply. 'But what else.... *exciting*, that is?'

– 'No – that's exactly it!' insisted Rico. 'The Bible and prayer!'

The storming of strongholds

Take it in. By concerted prayer – as we respond to what God tells us in the Bible – we are speaking back to Him, and so together engaging with the mightiest power in the universe. The English preacher Alfred Rowland once declared, *'Heaven fights for those who pray!'*

'Evangelism', writes Michael Green, 'involves storming strongholds. But a frontal assault is often useless. What is needed is tunnelling. That requires *hard work, sustained work, teamwork!* Such work is unseen and unsung. But it is crucial if the fortress is to be taken'(*New Life, New Lifestyle*, IVP).

Some Christian pioneers in a certain country discovered that, as new churches became established and bells began to ring on a Sunday, the powers of evil and witchcraft retreated. It was not that the evil powers were afraid of a bell, but rather of what the bell signified; the gathering of Christ's people for prayer. We should take to heart the vital pieces of armour against which satanic powers cannot stand; the Name of Christ, the Word of Christ, the Blood of Christ.... and the prayers of Christ's people.

So how is your Prayer Meeting these days?

Your church could touch the world

Joint, united prayer is axiomatic in the work we are given to do on earth. It is the divinely appointed way by which we co-operate with the mission of Christ. The power of prayer crosses barbed wire, leaps over oceans, penetrates prison walls. We pray; God works! Let us not murmur 'Oh, people can pray at home!' The united meeting for prayer in any locality is essential to a living church. *If your fellowship does not have a regular gathering for united prayer, begin one this week.* Once begun, your church could touch the world. Without such prayer, you will not be noticed much beyond your walls, let alone reach precious souls.

And how would a praying church be described? A first suggestion:

A praying church is a school of prayer

So much to learn! We read in 1 Timothy 2:1-4 of four types of prayer. First, there are *requests*, or 'entreaties'; that is, heartfelt pleas to God, particularly when a church is up against big challenges and we fling ourselves upon the Lord. Secondly, there are *prayers*; the word implies the general obtaining of good things from above. Thirdly we use *intercessions* – that is, the praying on behalf of people and situations. Fourthly, we have *thanksgivings*, from the Greek word *eucharistia*; these are the praises and thanks that are integral to the life of a church.

All four strands featured in the early church – to such an extent that, when an official ban was pronounced against all preaching of Jesus, the resulting prayer meeting was one of joyous praise, in which prayers were made, not for protection but for increasing **boldness.** It amounted to 'More of the same, please!' (Acts 4:18-31).

Steps towards an apostolic emphasis

If in any way our fellowships have lapsed in the central place given to united prayer, there are certain practical steps we can begin to take, by which we can recover something of the apostolic emphasis.

- First, the meeting for prayer is best held on a day and at a time *when nothing else is being arranged in the church.* This profile establishes the prayer meeting as the most important event of the week. It is best not scheduled as 'Bible Study and Prayer' for this risks reducing the significance of *both* activities.

- Second, let it be publicly known that the leader of the fellowship always presides at the prayer meeting – and that all other team members are present – *and will take no other local, simultaneous ministry assignments.* It won't be long before the top priority of the prayer meeting becomes apparent to all.

- Third, in appointing any voluntary workers in the fellowship (youth leaders, children's workers, home group hosts, Sunday welcomers, street pastors), the question should first be put, **'As one of the serving team, will you pledge yourself to be at the regular prayer meeting?'** If the answer is 'Well, I wouldn't have time for both,' then the reaction should perhaps be, 'Let's delay, then, until you *do* have time.' In this way, consistency with true spiritual priorities is recognised from the start, however limiting to 'the work' this may seem to be. *For prayer IS the work.* Naturally, parents with families might need to alternate in their attendance.

- Fourthly, when it comes to the annual election of officers, the membership should be publicly encouraged to nominate none other than *attenders at the prayer meeting.*

These are some of the lessons that can slowly be learnt in this school of prayer. *Eventually the health of a fellowship is accurately gauged, not by the turnout on Sundays so much as by the strength of the prayer gathering.*

A praying church is a cornershop of prayer

Back to the model of chapter four! The apostle Paul had urged for prayer: 'that we may live peaceful and quiet lives in all godliness and holiness'. *Peaceful and quiet lives in a community* – that is a natural by-product of a praying church. The corner-shop mindset of intimacy and service, with the arrows of concern pointing ever outwards to nearby families and local issues, cannot fail to impact the surrounding neighbourhood.

In an earlier ministry, Michael Baughen – my predecessor at London's All Souls Church – had led a growing work at Holy Trinity Church, in Platt Lane, Manchester. There, in the united prayer gathering, *actual roads and thoroughfares were named before God.*

'After a while,' reported Michael, 'we became aware of individuals and whole families arriving among us, from hitherto untouched streets that had featured in our prayers.' The church on the corner of Platt Lane was getting better and better known by the nearby residents.

Prayer is the first thing to go

Of course, it is all hard work! Dedication to prayer for people and situations is demanding. 'Do not omit the ministry of music!' George Verwer aptly urges in his chapter on prayer meetings *(Drops from a Leaking Tap*; Authentic, India*)*. Certainly, a music band can be playing as members arrive, and an hour and a half of prayer can be refreshingly interspersed by songs of praise.

But beware! *Actual intercession is about the first thing to go.* All too easily it becomes outflanked by twenty minutes of introductory worship songs, by reports, interviews, over-long DVDs and testimonies. And this happens because of a failure ever to have understood the privilege, and indeed delight, of being before the throne of God in a gathering at which Christ has pledged to be present. A professional dancer exclaimed to me once, 'I love the prayer gathering. It's the best night of all!'

As we pray, confidence builds. At the very least, those present can expectantly believe, as Sunday approaches, *We prayed about this. We asked that Sunday may be irradiated with glory!*

We must realise too that the fellowship, by its prayers, has the added privilege of touching *the world!* And so:

A praying church is a website of prayer

Leaders of 'larger churches' are sometimes asked, 'Do you aspire to be a mega church?' The answer ought always to be, No. *Far more important is for every church on earth, big or small, to aspire after being **a world church!*** For once again, on looking at 1 Timothy 2:1-4, the assumption is one of influence that stretches to the ends; the scope of our prayers are 'for everyone…. for kings…. all those in authority…. all men to be saved….'

The church, then, is to be like a world website on the Internet – with cyber-like threads of prayer, reaching to 'Jerusalem, and in all Judea and Samaria, and to the ends of the earth' (Acts 1:8).

Putting in some shape

Perhaps legitimately, we start with ourselves – 'Jerusalem'. After a welcome song, followed by prayers of thanksgiving and praise, and a short Bible talk (of no more than 3-5 minutes), we can indeed open up with local items, church organisations and forthcoming evangelistic events. And even in a large meeting, members can be invited to pray aloud – with a little coaching from the front!

'Keep the little voice UP if you can – without straining! And leave room for others, by keeping it SHORT!.... Don't worry if someone else collides with your prayer; I can always help with a bit of umpiring!.... It's just as spiritual to pray silently. But no need to worry about correct phraseology....'

Dividing into small groups

Variation is further achieved halfway through, by dividing the gathering into small praying groups of no more than four or five per group. The members can introduce themselves to each other and appoint their own leader.

Perhaps at that stage comes the opportunity of focusing internationally on the vital work of missionaries and the persecuted world. Has someone been appointed to harness the necessary information, perhaps with a short DVD or with photographs on PowerPoint? To brief a visiting missionary for a slot? To prepare a printed sheet for members to take away?

Naturally, time erodes when others step up front! We've all seen it happen. Someone is given three minutes. Inevitably this becomes eight. **We leaders have to work at this.** Once, in a big gathering, the flowers hid me as I dropped down to crawl across the stage and tug at the spokesman's trouser leg. It matters not in those countries, where no trains or buses have to be caught. In the West, however – although the missionary-faithful are oblivious to time – it is wise to end smack on the dot! To fail here is a fairly strong guarantee of attendance dwindling as weeks go by.

Final tips: Space the chairs out attractively. Keep it lively! Keep it cheerful, non-spooky and not so 'spiritual' that fewer numbers will come back next time!

FURTHER READING: *Talking about Prayer* by Richard Bewes, Christian Focus Publications; new imprint 2013.

9

The Jason Factor:

The Small Group

'See that tree over there? That's a church!' John Mpayeii was driving me beyond Kenya's famous *Ngong Hills* into Maasai territory.... and I was thrilled. As a child of missionaries, I had never got near the Maasai people – noted for their insularity and disdain of anything outside their cattle economy. My Dad had been in hundreds of Kikuyu dwellings, but never into a single Maasai homestead.

But the breakthrough for Jesus Christ had taken place, and it had happened supremely through years of prayer and long-suffering patience on the part of John Mpayeii, himself part Kikuyu and part Maasai. Now whole villages had become Christian.

'Look, there's another tree!' exclaimed John. 'That's a church too! You see,' he explained, 'Sunday by Sunday these Maasai worshippers of Jesus take it in turns; *You can all come to my tree next week.*'

It was a little like the early New Testament. In Europe it had started with just a riverside in the Gentile city of Philippi:

On the Sabbath we went outside the city gate to the river, where we expected to find a place of prayer. We sat down and began to speak to the women who had gathered there. One of those listening was a woman named Lydia, a dealer in purple cloth from the city of Thyatira, who was a worshipper of God. The Lord opened her heart to respond to Paul's message. When she and the members of her household were baptised, she invited us to her home. 'If you consider me a believer in the Lord,' she said, 'come and stay at my house.' (Acts 16:13–15)

So John Mpayeii seemed to be the first among the Maasai, just as Lydia was the first in Europe. Then there was Thessalonica, about 150 miles west of Philippi. Who was the first Christian there? It seems to have been Jason. It was not then by a riverside that Paul preached Jesus, but in the city's sole Jewish synagogue. Numbers of citizens believed.

Turning the world upside down

Then trouble broke out, just as it had done in Philippi. City-wide rage focused on the house of Jason. The complaint – graphically put in the King James Bible – was of *'These that have turned the world upside down'* (Acts 17:6, KJV). Paul and Silas had to quit town. Jason stayed put.

Really? Such reaction? And all provoked by a solitary home group in a great city? True, any household that has the equivalent of Paul and Silas staying and ministering there is likely to make itself known outside! But still…. could modern home groups be similarly powerful?

The answer is Yes. During the years when communism controlled parts of north Africa, a certain church denomination was officially shut down. No church services were permitted. At the time of the closure, the church had about 5,000 members. But within a few short years, the church numbered 50,000 — *without a single church service being held*. Home meetings had been the key.

'They are the key!' emphasised the Argentine evangelist Luis Palau one day to me. 'Of course, ideally we need the *teaching*. Without that, however effective the one-to-one evangelism may be, any unconnected network of home groups will eventually plateau or simply fade. The best pattern', said Luis, 'is that of a mother church, *surrounded* by ten, a dozen satellites. That way the teaching from the centre is preserved — *and multiplied!'*

John Wesley's 'classes'

The point is well taken. Certainly the New Testament gospel became rooted in people's homes — that of Lydia.... the town jailer.... Jason.... Aquila and Priscilla.... Crispus.... Paul's rented house.... and even in the household of Caesar himself (Phil. 4:22). But inevitably their very identity derived from the wider work of the apostles, from the church at large. The evangelist John Wesley knew of this successful pattern back in the eighteenth century, as he rode to towns and villages in his remarkable establishing of the 'societies' or 'class meetings' that became connected with wider Methodism.

Whenever in history the vision of small groups has been recaptured, the work can be expected to advance! It happened in seventeenth-century England. Across the country, men and women were studying the Scriptures in their homes, and the effect was marked. Of the seventeenth century, the great historian G.M. Trevelyan observed that the effect of the study of the Bible

> upon the national character, imagination and intelligence for nearly three centuries to come was greater than that of any literary movement in our annals or any religious

movement since the coming of St Augustine. (*History of England*, Longman's, Green & Co, 2nd edition, 1942, p. 367)

As great numbers of working people began to read the Bible for themselves, so literacy grew across the nation – and with it, social and economic development. The trade union movement was to owe much of its rise to Methodism.

More than a club
It was the Bible that did it. The power lies there. People were not meeting each other simply to discuss the political scene, or the price of corn. When joint study of the Bible is the point of focus, that small group becomes a living unit, and an integral part in the building of Christ's church.

But accountability to the greater body is vital. In this way, internal problems and questions can be raised, and counsel taken together, as happened with the massive issue of Gentile involvement, at the Council of Jerusalem (Acts 15). A group that subsists only within its own walls – as a solitary club of like-minded members – may well end up as an ineffective and isolated igloo on the icy wastes of surrounding paganism. Any chance of engaging with society in the public square is reduced to zilch.

It is the wider fellowship that gives identity to its satellite groups, imparting training to the leaders and making supportive visits.

Finding the resources
Lack of time is often the problem that voluntary group leaders struggle with. Again it is the mother body that, through experienced leadership, can provide courses of Bible study – complete with leaders' notes – common to every group. Further, it can make for unity all round, when Bible studies are tied in with current teaching at the church

centre. Better this, perhaps, than individual groups opting for their own internally chosen pet themes and passages.

'I was at my wits' end,' reported a church minister in East Anglia. 'We had virtually no trained leaders in the church, and every new venture that I suggested for our life together was turned down by the church council, with the comment *"We've tried that before and it never worked".*

'One day a brochure popped on to my doormat. It highlighted a group video Bible course entitled *Open Home, Open Bible*[1] – with study guides accompanying each 15-minute video. I played one of the videos at the church council, and the members said, "Seeing we have no trained leaders among us, this might work. Anyone can switch on a video machine, and presumably anyone can then open Bibles and look at the printed questions in the study guides. *This looks as though it can run itself.* Let's give it a try."'

A few months passed. The minister was later to report, 'From no home groups at all, we now have ten, and altogether we have 120 people studying the Bible, and saying, "Don't stop the programmes; we want more!" And now we have self-trained leaders!'

Whether with videos (now DVDs), or simply with published or home-devised programmes, the potential of small satellite groups clustered around the mother body lies in this – that believing people are learning to dig out the truths of the Bible for themselves.

'They ate together'
I once said to a tutor at London's Oak Hill Theological College, 'Tell me some of the secrets of the early church's sensational growth.'

---

1   *Open Home, Open Bible,* www.trinityvision.co.uk For *Book by Book* studies: *www.biblicalframeworks.com*

'Easy!' he smiled. He turned to the close of Acts chapter 2. 'They ate together'! So, while Bible study is key, eating together generates trust and friendship. Further, *they prayed together*, and so learnt to carry one another's burdens and concerns. Modern-day small groups do well when they can 'adopt' an overseas missionary, taking in from letters received and sending out books, gifts or magazines.

Within a group we can learn to love one another, bear with one another and forgive one another in a way that is not so practically achievable in the setting of the larger fellowship. It is there that we get to know one another; habits, characters, weaknesses, and all.

'I hate my fellowship group,' a young student once told me. 'Can I change to another group?'

'Yes, of course you can,' I replied. 'We don't want anyone to be unhappy in their group. But I tell you what. *Try it out twice more.* Then, if you're still unhappy, we can do something different.'

A month later, we met again. 'How's the group going?' I asked. The answer was interesting.

'I *love* my fellowship group!'

That's growth too – learning to adapt, adjust and accommodate within a gathering of highly varying types of people.

The lesson of delegation
The small group. Many lessons are learnt from William Grimshaw, the tough, eighteenth-century preacher at Haworth Parish Church in Yorkshire. He organised his parish into roughly ten areas, and made sure that there were leaders mature enough as Christians to take charge of one each – and of the home groups that would be formed within them. For Grimshaw could not be everywhere at once. A mighty

revival broke out around Yorkshire, and many thousands of people were lastingly blessed. To a great extent, it was the ministry in the homes that brought this about.

So when you hear it said in your area, 'I want to see the minister – the rector!' – it may fall in the end to a selected and trained home group leader to act as a church elder and be the one who gives pastoral counsel and ministry within the smaller fellowship. If a member of the group falls ill, it need not necessarily be one of the church staff who makes the hospital visit, but instead one or more members of the group who go, equipped with the Bible – and grapes.

Story of a Day of Prayer

I knew a young family, in which the youngest child was very gravely ill and pronounced beyond recovery. It was the members of their fellowship group who suggested a Day of Prayer for the entire group. They chose a Saturday, and began with breakfast together. Prayer followed. Then midmorning coffee. Again, prayer. Then came lunch…. and further prayer. Tea was provided in the afternoon, and once more the group prayed.

The doctors were dumbfounded at the little girl's resulting recovery. Nothing was said publicly. The story was never publicised. Yet, I remember later seeing the toddler racing down the central aisle at the close of Sunday church…. and thanking the Lord God that he can use a young and mutually trusting bunch of everyday followers of Jesus to achieve His mighty works.

See that tree over there by the Ngong Hills? That riverbank in Philippi? That home in Thessalonica surrounded by a yelling mob? Those young Londoners meeting for breakfast?

Become part of the Jason Factor…. it's happening worldwide.

10

Group Study:
A Pool of Ignorance?

Not a day goes by when our Bible study group programmes, *Open Home, Open Bible* and *Book by Book*, are not seen on the small screen and in more countries than our own. And such is the wonder of modern technology that my colleague Paul Blackham and I – accompanied always by an international invited guest – may have our speaking 'dubbed' into another language.

'As far as the Germans are concerned,' says Paul, 'I much prefer the voice *you* were given to the one they gave *me*! Yours is rich and magisterial; mine seems to be on the high-pitched side!'

But at least the attempt is being made to inspire individual viewers and small groups everywhere to delve into real Bible study. **Not that we are doing the work *for* the viewers.** Our role is simply to engage in a fifteen-minute introductory discussion of a Bible passage, or a specific Bible truth, and so – with the help of available printed study guides – to stimulate our viewing friends to follow on and do further work for themselves.... in books such as John's Gospel, Exodus, 1 Peter, Ephesians, Nahum, Psalms, Revelation or Isaiah. And, in the case of *Open Home, Open Bible*, we delve into sixty major truths that run through Scripture, from Creation to the Last Things.

But that is to point to only two of many helps available to the thousands upon thousands of small groups that meet in churches, in student circles and even in prisons. The overriding concern is how to approach joint Bible study once a group has been established. And what is the task of the leader?

The power resides not in any media aid, nor in any personalities involved, *but in the Scriptures themselves.* You cannot get a group of people around the Bible and not expect the touch of God upon them. It is a cumulative exercise. Over the weeks that a small group meets in this way, the participants are steadily building up a godly, a Christ-centred way of looking at and interpreting *life.* It was through the Scriptures that the mindset of all Europe was changed centuries ago. Now, in what we in the West may excitingly describe as 'a new pre-Christian era', this is how a nation's thinking can be changed. Given enough determination, it can happen, from the grass roots upwards; in village after village, campus after campus, finally affecting the world of business, media, education and political leadership. *It is not the result of a mere whim that a group Bible study is regularly held in the British Houses of Parliament.*

The Bible will do it. How, then, to engage with it on a small-group level? Certainly DVDs can play a part, but they should never do the work for us. There comes a moment when, with introductions over, sitting perhaps on some student's threadbare strip of carpet with Bibles open and a can of Coke, participation begins. Perhaps *you* are the leader?

What are the dynamics of the group?

Let's get the dynamics right. **First, it is a group, not a congregation!** Nobody should be preaching or teaching from the front. The main duty of the leader is to kick-start the proceedings with a prayer and brief introduction, to encourage discussion and be ready to sum up at the close.

The ideal number for a group is around eight to twelve people. Effectiveness reduces once the group grows beyond that number. If yet others wish to join in Bible study, the group may need to divide – and this is the start of a new group…. provided someone is available to lead. And worry not, if you as leader fret at the poor extent of your Bible knowledge! *Do you love the Lord? Love people? You're hungry for the Bible? Are you reasonably at ease sitting and talking with others, even in a supposed pool of ignorance?* If so, you're probably in for a good time!

Secondly, the group is an organism, not a hotchpotch of individuals. Pray for your members, day by day. If the group can stay together for a recognizable period, trust and mutual care will develop. Concerns for each other's families will grow. Slowly, around you all, is developing a unit of spiritual LIFE.

Thirdly, it is a sharing, not a lecture. Again and again, leaders get this *wrong* – imagining that they must display their great learning. Not so; theirs is to be the difficult, but achievable, skill of keeping the ball rolling, and encouraging members to discover the truths for *themselves.* The more the group comes up with its *own* answers to the truth of a Bible passage, the more successful are you, the leader!

How should the room be arranged?
First, **with care and thought.** What are the dynamics operating on this occasion? You may be a sizeable crowd in a large auditorium, led initially from the front in a *plenary* 'introductory' session, perhaps with an on-screen presentation. Then comes a breaking up into smaller,

informal 'table groups' of six or eight members, each with its appointed co-ordinator.

Or is the occasion a small group study from the start? Don't organise a semi-circle with leader's chair at the front, for that would imply that all conversation should be directed to and from a *guru*-style leader. Better to aim for a not-too-tight-not-too-neat circle of chairs, of which the leader's is but one.

And a second tip: Let the room be arranged **with warmth and informality.** Just look around. The *lighting* needs to be good. And the room should be so prepared that the hosts really seem to *want* people to come! Would some gentle music help the atmosphere as members arrive?

A third tip – **with refreshment and hospitality**. Cultural customs vary even from city to city, but at the least, coffee can help at the start. *Warning:* Let not refreshments dominate over the importance of meeting around God's Word. And just remember; if you put on a full–scale meal at the close of the study, it may be some while before the last member leaves!

What makes a good Bible study?

At the agreed time, we get people seated, have the Bibles out and open with prayer. It is always possible to invite one of the group to pray, but the more nervous may fear that one day they may be 'pounced on' to do the same. It's tactful to say, 'I've already asked Bill if he would pray for us to understand the passage.'

Then the passage may be read aloud. The recommendation is not for members to read a verse in turn; it's too artificial, and for some very nerve-wracking. Let one member read – or two or three may volunteer to take separate sections.

And then?

'Great,' says the leader. 'Why don't we spend a minute or two looking at the passage, and see if we can work out its main theme? What do you think might be the *big* point coming across? There may even be some "sub-themes" here. Take a moment, everybody, and let's have a look.'

The one main message

Silence falls. As with the John Stott axiom (ch. 5), the guideline is to find out from the passage the *natural* meaning (without twisting the words), the *original* meaning (the one thing the writer of the passage was intending to say) and the *general* meaning (that would tie in with and harmonise with what the rest of Scripture says). Only later need the question of practical application arise.

After a minute or two, the leader breaks the silence. 'As we learnt last time, these words were written by the apostle Paul while he was in prison, probably around the year A.D. 50. At this point, what is he on about? What's the main thing he's trying to say to his readers? Have a go, someone!'

Someone speaks up and looks across to you as leader, for confirmation that they got it right.

Tip. Don't look back at them; no eye contact! Rather, look away — around the rest of the group — and ask, 'Hmmm; anyone else? Let's see what others think!' *Reason:* You are not to allow the rest of the group to cast you in the role of dominating, know-all teacher. All you are doing is encouraging the *others* to dig out the meaning of the passage for themselves. And the best way of doing it is by way of non-threatening questions.

Someone comes up with a contribution. You know that they are way off-course — but at least they made the attempt! So, rather than assert, 'No, I'm afraid you got that completely wrong,' they will be better helped by way of a gentle challenge: 'In saying that, Bob, which verse were you looking at there?' Little by little, the group gets the message: *We are here to discover what the writer was getting at, and therefore what God is saying.*

A study is going well when the members are not simply engaging with *you* but across the room *with each other.* The great skill of the leader is to interject stimulating questions. Most printed study-guides will actually suggest what questions may be appropriate to the Bible passage. Avoid questions that invite the answer Yes or No, and shun 'dumbing-down' questions that have all-too-obvious answers!

'As we look at verses 6-12, let's identify some of the descriptions Paul uses of the ministry he and his colleagues were carrying out' (1 Thess. 2:6-12). Plenty will emerge from such a question – *gentle like a mother.... sharing not only the gospel but our lives as well.... our toil and hardship.... night and day....not to be a burden.... holy, righteous and blameless .... as a father deals with his own children.*

The leader picks up again. 'In practical terms, what can be learnt from this about Christian standards of service *today*?' So now, we are veering into application. Bible study at its best poses **two questions**; first – from the past – *What did it mean?* And secondly - for today – *What does it say?* If we answer only the first question, we risk becoming anti-quarians. But if we skip the discipline of the first question and go straight to the second, we risk becoming existential-ists – only concerned with *experience.* Both exercises balance each other.

What are the pitfalls?

There certainly are a few! First, avoid **The one-man Show,** when the leader dominates all. This kills all learning. Secondly, there is **The great Silence.** It is, generally, the *right* question that breaks this. If the group is really 'sticky', members can always be invited initially to select a 'favourite verse.' Third, we can be struggling with **The Show-Off** – with his knowledge of Greek words! Later, he can be taken aside and affirmed in his knowledge, but be told that too much erudition only stifles discussion among others. Fourthly, **The Red Herring**; that is, diversion on to some side issue. The leader may have to say, 'We can take that up after coffee, Fred, but what about Paul's *main* point in verse 8?' Then there is **The Pet Theme** – whether it be church unity, millennial prophecies, the Jordanian valleys or vegetarianism. Ever been in **The Paper Chase** – with the member who is forever turning the pages with exhausting Bible cross-references? A little gentle umpiring may be called for: 'Great, Sue, but time may be against us. Keep it to the end if time permits. Back to verse 11 again?'

How do we end?

The leader does well to keep track of the key points established. If necessary, jot some of them down while the discussion proceeds. Then, as the study ends, these main truths and applications can be summarised, and – if prayer is to follow – can stimulate our praying.

If a member can come away with ONE mighty discovery made, that will be cause for praise!

Part Three:

One on One

One loving spirit sets another on fire.

AUGUSTINE OF HIPPO

A.D. 354–430

Confessions IV: 14, 21

One on One

11

'I Had a Friend'

In our family, as children, we had a stack of interests, but the favourite was tennis. I was to make scrapbooks, obtain autographs and eventually play in tournaments. Then one year, my parents took in the son of an overseas Christian missionary; he lived with us for many months. His name was Paul Wigram. Although not noted for his tennis interest, it was not long before the enthusiasm of the rest of us rubbed off on to him.

'Auntie Sylvia,' he confessed one day, 'I'm sorry, but I've broken an electric light bulb.'

– 'Never mind, Paul,' said my mum, 'we'll put in a new one. Which room was it in?'

– 'In the loo.'

– 'In the –' calmly, 'But how did you ever break it in there, of all places?'

– 'I'm sorry. I was just practising my serve!'

This is how the burning captivations that can take hold of a few become common on a wider front. They tend to rub off from one to another, whether in the impressionable world of sport, art or fashion, or simply through the fads that can sweep a school playground.

But Christianity was never a fad. Certainly there are deviations on the edge of the Christian faith or shallow belief based only on the experience of personal sensations. These will not survive the tests of time. Os Guinness has written, 'Those who once tripped on drugs and now trip on Jesus will find some new trip' (*The Dust of Death*, IVP).

Martyrs for the Truth

Thus, a feelings-only faith could never have produced the first Christians. Something had actually happened, and a Man had visibly lived among them – whose words were remembered, whose deeds were recalled and whose rising from the dead had been publicly witnessed. *Their view of existence and of the universe around them was permanently changed as a result.* So convinced were they, that thousands cheerfully went to their death as martyrs for the sake of the gospel that had so captivated them.

This was news of a living God who had revealed Himself in the God-Man Jesus. And – on the basis of the historical death of this Man on a hilltop outside Jerusalem – eternal salvation and a place in the eternal kingdom would be bestowed as a free gift to any who accepted this risen Christ. He was to be proclaimed as Conqueror of death, world Ruler, universal Saviour …. and daily Companion to all who followed Him along life's highway.

Result? There was an explosion of joy. The early believers could hold nothing back in their witness to Jesus. Naturally, there was going to be trouble. A Greek believer, Stephen, became the first martyr. The book of Acts tells us that on that very day a violent persecution broke out against the church, and that all except the apostles were scattered:

Those who had been scattered preached the word wherever they went. (Acts 8:4)

The releasing trigger

It could be argued that the killing of Stephen, and its aftermath, was – in the overruling providence of God – the unwitting trigger that despatched thousands of evangelists on to a one-to-one gossiping of the gospel along the 58,000 miles of highway that threaded the Roman empire. *It was the most natural way in which the new faith was going to grow!*

Sometimes Bible students have wondered why there are scarcely any exhortations in the New Testament letters to *evangelise.* Certainly Jesus had commanded His followers to make disciples of all nations, but little is said in the letters, beyond Paul's instruction in 2 Timothy 4:2, to 'preach the word'.

The reason is obvious. Witnessing to Christ and sharing the good news is axiomatic for the grateful believer who has received forgiveness through the Cross and who, by the power of the Spirit, is assured of His indwelling presence. We cannot but help wanting others to know!

'To bear witness'

Each generation of believers must take this in, afresh. The East African revival leader, Festo Kivengere, was present at the eleventh worldwide *Lambeth Conference* at Canterbury, attended by church leaders from all over the world. On the last afternoon, Festo publicly expressed his dismay that, in a debate on 'Gospel and Dialogue' no reference had been made to the action of reaching out to others in evangelism. This is what he moved as an amendment:

> *Dialogue can never be a substitute for proclamation. We therefore resolve ourselves to call on all our churches, to respond with greater obedience and commitment to our Lord's unfulfilled commission to bear witness to him and to make disciples.*

You know what? To the surprise and consternation of many African bishops, the amendment was narrowly defeated!

TIP: Don't rely on heavyweight pronouncements and procedural resolutions as to whether to move ahead in spreading the news of Jesus Christ – *but rather, get on with it yourself.* Others will follow your example, for evangelism is an 'infection' of the gospel! And the keys to one-to-one 'proclamation' are very simple:

The key of prayer
The American pastor Ronald Dunn once wrote of members of his congregation who would ask him to pray for their unbelieving spouses. Always he would agree, writing down the name, and his subsequent regular prayer request would be presented with the words: 'Make them hungry, Lord.' Time and again, he would then begin to witness a steady alteration from unbelief to faith (*Don't Just Stand There; Pray Something!* Thomas Nelson publishers).

A brilliant lay evangelist, Vijay Menon, of India, had never even seen a Bible until one day he inadvertently walked into a service at the London church of St Helen's, Bishopsgate. 'I went into that place a total non-Christian', he told me, 'and forty minutes later came out as a Christian! But then,' he added, 'with such a rapid turnaround in my soul, I later began to think that someone must have been praying for me – but I couldn't think who it was.'

Seven long years
Then it transpired that it was his English landlady in London, *the only Christian he knew.* Shy of witnessing verbally to a male lodger of another country and another belief, she had given herself to daily prayer for Vijay. This she had maintained for seven long years. The answer from heaven, when it finally came, was instant and dramatic.

It starts with prayer. The apostle Paul commends praying for others with the words, 'This is good, and pleases God our Saviour, who wants all men to be saved and to come to a knowledge of the truth' (1 Tim. 2:3-4). We can be sure, then, that we are in harmony with the desires of heaven itself when prayer of this kind is offered.

The key of friendship
I was programme chairman of a Billy Graham youth event in Brussels years ago, when we, the organisers, put out a questionnaire among the eight thousand delegates. One of the questions was, *What was the main factor behind your coming to faith in Jesus Christ?* We had then listed some twenty or so possibilities.

Easily top of the answers given was *The friendship of a Christian.* Far and away at the bottom were two items: *The giving of a pamphlet* and *The witness of a stranger.*

Naturally, there are many instances when the giving of a Christian tract, or words spoken by a stranger, have brought a positive response. But there is something about the impact of a friend that is 'incarnational'. The Lord God did not simply drop words from heaven in His mission to our dying world. He came *in Person....* and Jesus was forever going into people's homes, eating with them, receiving, giving – and opening up the very love of God in friendship.

Time after time I have asked those new to belief how it was that they ever came into the orbit of the church, the Bible, prayer and worship. 'Oh,' they will say, 'I had a friend'. In no way does this factor negate the importance of big arena missions or festivals *for the majority of those who come to such events are brought by a friend.* Mass outreach is, by its very nature, friendship outreach.

The key of trust
When trust exists, there is no need for two individuals forever to be avoiding mutual offence by skirting carefully and

tactfully round each other. When there is trust between friends, they can speak as they wish.

Yet there are some believers of a shy and retiring disposition who question inwardly whether they have 'the gift' of sharing their belief at all. In point of fact, it is frequently the shyer among us who prove to be as effective as any.... and perhaps this is because they seem unthreatening, *and therefore approachable.*

Towards the end of the eighteenth century William Wilberforce achieved world prominence, in championing the abolition of the slave trade. But 1785 found him anxiously in search of a living faith, at the age of twenty-six. Whom could he trust with this very personal quest? Eventually he picked the sixty-year-old John Newton, then rector of the London city church of St Mary Woolnoth – experiencing, as he put it, 'ten thousand doubts' about making the visit at all.

Wilberforce took precautions to prevent whispering among his friends. He begged Newton to maintain secrecy about the visit. He walked twice round Charles Square in Hoxton, before he could bring himself to knock on Newton's door at the appointed time. But in Newton he had chosen well; Wilberforce was eventually to become a vital member of one of the most effective reforming churches in Christian history – Holy Trinity, Clapham (See *John Venn and the Clapham Sect*, by Michael Hennell, Lutterworth Press).

The key of God's glory

Why bother at all about making Christ known to as many people as possible? The supreme reason is the glory of God. We read of the distress that the apostle Paul experienced on his arrival at Athens, which was infinitely more pluralist in its religious beliefs than anything we can encounter in today's Western cities. Initially dismissed by the local philosophers as a 'babbler', he eventually is invited to speak at the city's most prestigious institution, the Areopagus.

And there Paul's cue is given to him by the existence of a heathen altar dedicated to 'An Unknown God' – erected presumably as an insurance against the offence that some anonymous deity might take at not being identified. Paul then addresses the ignorance of the Athenians, as he proclaims the one, true and universal God:

> In the past God overlooked such ignorance, but now he commands all people everywhere to repent. For he has set a day when he will judge the world with justice by the man he has appointed. He has given proof of this to all men by raising him from the dead. (Acts 17:30, 31)

Paul was met with laughter by some. They might not have laughed so readily had they known that their nearby temple of the Parthenon – looking as beautiful as though its marble columns had been set up the day before instead of four hundred years earlier – would one day become a Christian church, and a church it remained for a thousand years.

Paul's message left no room for the thought that the human race is on a journey to some mountain top – and that all roads would eventually lead there. It was vital for his listeners to understand that there is only one road, and that Christ is the only way to the living and true God. *There can be many roads to Christ, but Christ is the only road to God.*

It is for the sake of the name and glory of God in Jesus Christ that men and woman down the ages have made it their business to make Him known – by prayer, example, friendship and word – to people they meet and know.

Is that how it has happened for you?

12

No Proselytism
Here Please!

It was a leader from the Middle East, of another belief, who was complaining to me sharply about the mission activities of a Christian student group in a British university. The adherents of his own religion in the college, he claimed, resented having to stand up to the claims of Christ that they were hearing – and requested that the Christians be told to stop 'proselytising.'

As I talked with him, it became apparent that he was unaware of several important issues in the realm of ideas. First, he seemed oblivious to the cherished principle of free speech in a democracy such as Britain's. The exchange and challenging of ideas is always to be encouraged, especially in the universities, where they are an essential part of a student's developing mindset.

Secondly, he was referring to evangelism – an activity by which many religions (including his own) propagate their own beliefs worldwide – but describing it in its *Christian* form by the deliberately insulting term 'proselytism'. Evangelism and proselytism are not the same, and it was obviously important that this critic should be made clearly to understand the difference. Do you know the difference yourself?

The term 'proselytisers' is tossed around the world of journalism and philosophy, and is almost entirely applied to Christians, whose joyful privilege it is to communicate and share the news of the living Christ with friends and neighbours. Why are such Christians *not* proselytisers? The distinction between evangelism and proselytism needs to be clarified.

It was the certain religious leaders of His own time whom Jesus described scathingly as proselytisers:

> *Woe unto you, scribes and Pharisees, hypocrites! For ye compass sea and land to make one proselyte, and when he is made, ye make him twofold more the child of hell than yourselves* (Matt. 23:15, KJV)

Every art of persuasion

The word *proselyte*, from the King James Version, is a more preferable translation of the Greek *proseelutos*, than the blander word *convert*, used in the New International Version. Although a proselyte was indeed a Gentile recruit won for Judaism, the process was not an attractive one. The Jewish historian Josephus tells us of John Hyrcanus, a military commander, civil governor and high priest of Judea from 134–104 B.C. At one point, he offered the Idumeans (a people he had conquered) the alternative of death or conversion to Judaism…. which would have included circumcision. Later, when the growing power of Rome made such extreme measures illegal, *every other possible art of persuasion was attempted.*

All too frequently the result was extremely low-grade 'converts' – in Jesus' estimation, twice as hell-bound as their masters. It even became a saying that no one should trust a proselyte, even to the twenty-fourth generation. As the German theologian H.J. Holtzmann put it, 'the more converted, the more perverted'.

Basically, it is 'Unworthy Witness' that distinguishes proselytism from evangelism. A useful international church study document entitled 'Common Witness and Proselytism' was produced some decades ago. It declared that there were several sides to witness that should be described as unworthy of Christ. First, there are:

Unworthy motives

A variety of 'unworthy motives' lay behind the activities of many religious leaders during Jesus' ministry in Judea, and we can recognise them in our own era. **Pride and a jealous obsession with power** are often foremost. This was apparent among the Pharisees. Their unrivalled monopoly of influence came under threat when the crowds flocked to hear Christ and witness His authority. Later, in their own turn, Peter and the apostles were jailed, out of similar jealousy (Acts 5:17-28). Sectarian pride and religious 'power' are a negation of the Cross. In more recent times, I recall turning the pages of a prominent evangelist's monthly magazine containing no fewer than seventeen photographs of himself. The opening sentence read, 'My report is given by three men; the prophet Isaiah, the apostle Peter, *and myself*'!

The other major unworthy motive that turns Christian witnesses into proselytisers is **concern for self-glory** rather than for the kingdom of God. It is then that individuals or churches unwittingly become self-promoting and self-regarding 'sectarian' bodies, indifferent to others in the wider family of Christ. Prayer may take place but is oblivious to activity and ministry beyond its own circle. The overpowering desire – like that of the Pharisees of old – is to draw recruits exclusively into its own clique, period. A second negative feature of proselytism concerns:

Unworthy methods

Christian missionaries have always had to remind each other never to produce 'Rice-Christians' from their labours, lest all they have bred were disciples tantalised into belief with the lure of full stomachs, clothing and money.

Yet today 'The Prosperity Gospel' is in full swing.... everywhere. To hold, as many do, that the true believer can expect a better car, salary increase and glowing good health is easily done – and falls directly into the pit of proselytism. It is not even short-term Christianity; it is not Christianity at all. Yet I have read the words of a certain evangelist, who placed two Bible texts neatly against each other:

> **Deuteronomy: 28:11** – 'The Lord will grant you abundant prosperity – in the fruit of your womb, the young of your livestock and the crops of your ground – in the land he swore to your forefathers to give you.'

And then....

> **Hebrews 7:22** – '...Jesus has become the guarantee of a better covenant.'

I quote the evangelist's words: *'If it was the will of God for men and woman to prosper then, how much more under the New Covenant!'* That was the argument: extra wealth, if you believe in Jesus.

Answers to the Prosperity Gospel

Some people may believe such a message, but, emphatically, no one is believing it – or preaching it – in the southern Sudan, in Iran, in Haiti, North Korea or in Nairobi's shanty town of Pumwani. *Christianity promises no material or physical insurance policy.* Read on from Hebrews chapter 7! The whole point about the key word *better* in the Letter to the Hebrews is that the New Covenant – centred in the once-for-all sacrifice of Christ at the Cross – brings *every* believer everlasting forgiveness, immediate access to the throne of God and into a superior DIMENSION of covenant blessings altogether. It embraces believers in Beijing, Calais, Buenos Aires, Calcutta, Perth or Mogadishu!

Garth Hewitt in his album *The Road to Freedom*, sang these timely words:

> I see those TV preachers;
> holy get-you-rich-quick teachers,
> Like pre-digested TV dinners,
> offer instant salvation packs for sinners;
> 'Put your hand on the TV screen'
> makes God look like a slot machine.
> Is this really what you meant
> by your costly blood-bought Covenant?

It is not just the offer of material benefits that turns Christian witness into proselytism. Other methods that are unworthy of the gospel will include the psychological pressure of verbal coercion, manipulating techniques **or indeed even blind force.** Christ's veto of the sword ruled out for ever the way of the Crusades, the Spanish Inquisition, the holy war or the Jihad. *Resorting to violence is a clear admission that you've lost the argument.* The evangelism of the true disciple is to be marked for ever by the love of our enemies.

Bribery, coercion or force all add up to unworthy methods in our evangelistic enterprises.

An unworthy message
Here is a third mark of proselytisers. It is that of distorting either their own message or that of their competitors, to meet a desired result. Regarding their own message, they may even be 90 per cent close to biblical standards, but it is so often what they have chosen *not* to teach that identifies them. In the New

Testament letter of Jude – written between A.D. 65 and 80 by one of Jesus' four half-brothers – we are taken on a tour of a spiritual disaster area.

Jude's problem with diversionist teachers was that they can sound so sensationally plausible.... and we know this today. The word gets around: 'Listen to this incredible CD! Watch that amazing programme! Come and hear this sensational preacher!' There comes a point when a church leader will declare, *'Well yes, I thank God for the spiritual roots that first got me established... but now I've moved on.'*

Biblically, the only way to 'move on' is to move back – to the granite foundations of 'the faith that was *once and for all* entrusted to the saints' (Jude 3) – and to dig ever deeper into them. Without them, what happens is that the extremes of yesterday become the norms of today. Jude himself was only too aware of this as he wrote of those who were embracing an unworthy message:

> Woe to them! They have taken the way of Cain; they have rushed for profit into Balaam's error; they have been destroyed in Korah's rebellion. These men are blemishes at your love-feasts, eating with you without the slightest qualm – shepherds who feed only themselves. They are clouds without rain, blown along by the wind; autumn trees without fruit and uprooted – twice dead. They are wild waves of the sea, foaming up their shame; wandering stars, for whom blackest darkness has been reserved for ever. (Jude 11-13)

Three examples are given. There was *Cain*, concerned only for his own fortunes. There was the Mesopotamian prophet *Balaam*, who finally proved to be no more than a compromising careerist (Num. 22–24; 2 Pet. 2:15, 16; Rev. 2:14). *Korah* also is named – his message revolved around a power-kick of his own creation (Num. 16:1-3).

Distortion of the truth

There is another side to the 'Unworthy Message' report from the church statement on proselytism. Proselytisers may also be identified by their tactic of deliberately distorting, not only their own message, but that of whom they think of as rivals. This has been done to many faithful servants of Christ down the centuries. The outstanding Christian leader, Athanasius, suffered terribly in this respect sixteen centuries ago, and was even exiled, as a result of such attacks.

John Wesley's detractors in the eighteenth century would write colourful tracts against him. *A full discovery of the horrid blasphemies taught by those Diabolical Seducers called Methodists* was the title of one article. *The Full Portrait of that frightful monster called Methodism* was another. Wesley and his colleagues were described as *furious disciples of Antichrist, reverend scavengers, filthy pests and plagues of mankind.* Wesley was 'grossly immoral', a Jesuit in disguise; a traitor, secretly raising troops for the King of Spain.

But have we ever acted like this? The warning to us is strong. If Jesus pronounced the self-serving proselytisers and their recruits of his own time as children of hell, it is little wonder that Jude used similar language.

The right view of Evangelism

By way of correction against proselytism, we need a right view of evangelism, and for this we can hardly do better than go to a declaration issued by another conference – hosted by the Billy Graham organisation in Manila in 1989, at the International Congress on World Evangelisation. This report argued for the Christian witness....

> ... to make an open and honest statement of (the gospel), which leaves the hearers entirely free to make up their own

minds about it. We wish to be sensitive to those of other faiths, and so we reject any approach that seeks to force conversion on them.

Learn this distinction between evangelism and proselytism, and keep it in mind. For make no mistake, one day we are going to need it!

And…. we can take action about proselytism. *Jude says so.* '**Build yourselves** up in your most holy faith and pray in the Holy Spirit. **Keep yourselves** in God's love as you wait for the mercy of our Lord Jesus Christ to bring you eternal life. **Be merciful** to those who doubt; **snatch others from the fire** and save them' (vv. 20-23).

Act on advice from a seventeenth-century Puritan, Richard Baxter:

'We should so lay the foundation of truth that error will fall by itself.'

13

The Art
of Creating Doubt

A journalist once asked the Christian singing troubadour, Garth Hewitt, what his aim was on stage, when singing to a largely secular audience.

'I feel I'm up there', replied Garth, *'mainly to create doubt –* in the mind of the ardent unbeliever. By my lyrics, by my in-between comments, I'm largely on an undermining mission.'

Naturally, in the hearts of Christians shines the burning desire that the dying world around us shall be won to outright faith in Jesus Christ. But there may have to be an earlier stage in the progression from unbelief to faith. That is where Garth Hewitt was operating – as also was the ancient writer of the book of Ecclesiastes, confronted by his own era of cynical indifference:

> I denied myself nothing my eyes desired; I refused my heart no pleasure. My heart took delight in all my work, and this was the reward for all my labour. Yet when I surveyed all that my hands had done and what I had toiled to achieve, everything was meaningless, a chasing after the wind; nothing was gained under the sun. (Eccles. 2:10, 11)

The book of Ecclesiastes derives from King David's son, the renowned Solomon (Eccles. 1:1). It presents us with an inspired critique of life that has become secularised and devoid of faith in God. Solomon had tried everything: intellectual pursuits, entertainment, drinking, big buildings, horticulture, vast employment, massive wealth and exotic women. In the end, everything seemed meaningless.

Dancing to a tune?

The book of Ecclesiastes is pushing and teasing its readers all along the line – and goading them into thinking…. and asking *questions*. Even in the romantic third chapter on 'A time for everything', there lurks – in the round of seasons and activities – the searching question for the reader, *In life without God, are we being made to dance to a tune?* Today, it may be the tune of the endless flow of text messages, or the iPad crammed with apps; it may be the dance routine of twenty-first century backpackers who have successfully *been there and done that.* All conceivable boxes have been ticked, but none of them were ever marked, 'Building my Character', 'Knowing my purpose in Life' or 'Establishing my Relationship to the Universe'. Ecclesiastes is there in the Bible to show that it is possible to be everywhere – and nowhere.

The writer and columnist Matthew Parris spelt it out most honestly in a book of his:

> 10,000 constituency letters answered, 3,000 newspaper columns written, 2,000 parliamentary sketch columns, 200 reviews of morning papers on TV, 100 hours of interviews on *Weekend World,* fifty Party Conferences, nine books, seven General Elections.
>
> …. All done, gone, knocked off and finished…. How much anxiety, how much hope and intelligence flares through the

night like a fire blazing unwatched under the cold stars, illuminating nothing, warming no one. Flames leap…. but they are earthbound…. (*Chance Witness*, Penguin 2002, p. 485)

Let the book of Ecclesiastes help any of us in today's materialistic world, desiring to share our belief with another – naturally and in friendship. For the writer is on our side! Although he deliberately adopts the stance of an unbeliever, from time to time he gives us a tiny hint and reveals his colours. He will pull the curtain back a little, voicing the suspicion that after all there is more to life than the mere fluctuation of seasons and systems (Eccles. 3:11). But his process is one of the raising of genuine questions. That can be our part too.

The part played by friendly curiosity

Who are your friends? Do they share your interests? Are they at work? Are they into sport, fashion, films, politics? Do they have any religious beliefs at all? Or maybe some form of New Age teaching ? Are they from another belief altogether than your own? Our curiosity about their perception of life and its meaning can very naturally open the door to any serious discussion you may embark upon together.

With friends from a different religion, an obvious question is, 'In your own beliefs, *how does someone get forgiven?*' Only a few years ago in Egypt, a national newspaper survey was set up across the country, with a single question: *What do you desire above everything else in life?* The top answer from the largely Muslim population was, 'To know that I am forgiven.' For many it is a massive concern.

The meaning of life?
Forgiveness will not necessarily surface as a top personal issue in the West. But for many – although serious self-questioning may be buried underground by non-stop

activity and driving ambitions – the question can still be uneasily present about the meaning of life. It is not so much the question 'What is the truth?' as it might have been a hundred years ago; rather, *'What is the point?'* The extensive diary of a well-known and successful British entertainer was published after his death in the 1990s:

> *August 22nd*: I wonder if anyone will ever know about the emptiness of my life? I wonder if anyone will ever stand in a room that I have lived in, and touch the things that were once a part of my life, and ask themselves what manner of man I was. How to ever tell them? How to ever explain?

A question that can help us to understand a friend's mindset is, 'How would you describe your worldview – your basic belief about life? What keeps you ticking?' It is no answer to reply, 'Actually, I have no worldview.' Every man, woman and child on earth has some perception as to what life here is all about. Nor is 'Well, I'm an atheist' any kind of answer. We are not asking our friends what they *don't* believe, but what they *do* believe about the meaning and purpose of their existence.

Four mighty planks
TIP: Be sure to have done some thinking on your own world-view! Be aware of the four major truths that undergird the whole teaching of the Bible: *Creation, the Fall, Redemption through the Cross and the final Triumph at the return of Christ.* In our minds, we are constantly assembling a raft with which we can negotiate the rocks and currents of modern thought. From the centre of our raft rises a mast, topped by an ensign labelled *Jesus Christ* – the apex, goal and pivotal centre of all that shapes our thinking. And the four Truths are like four mighty planks that make up our raft. As we get these firmly into place, we will soon find that we have a handle on every

issue going. We will have something to say about humanity, sport, wealth creation, death, politics, art, race, sex, conflict, education, suffering, the family, and a whole deal more. We can speak into any one of these topics from one or other of the mighty planks – sometimes indeed from all four.

To discuss each other's worldview, with no holds barred, is a product of trusting friendship. It usefully tests the Christian's own convictions, but it also can pose a challenge to the non-believer by creating doubt about a worldview that cannot credibly hold together. Our part is that of friendly curiosity. But there is another side to this.

The part played by prayerful patience

A statue stands today, on Washington's Capitol Hill of Lew Wallace, known in the mid-nineteenth century as a prominent American major general and later as Governor of Utah. As an author, Wallace declared to his wife that he intended to examine the New Testament – with a view to exploding what he felt to be the myth of Christ's resurrection. Wisely, his praying wife kept her own counsel and waited.

Lew Wallace's research led him irresistibly to the conclusion that the story of the Gospels could not be disproved, and belief grew in him. He confided to his wife that the book could not, after all, be written. She persuaded him to the contrary. The book could still be written…. but from a different standpoint altogether. *Ben Hur: A Tale of the Christ* was the result. It has never been out of print from 1880 until today.

The value of prayer and ongoing patience has been well proved when believing people have been faced by the prejudices, materialism and sheer busyness that keep God out of the thinking of their friends. We should resist the mental temptation to consign the sceptics prematurely to the pit of their own making. The Psalmist of old refers to 'a pit that is dug for the wicked'. But Augustine of old, in his comment on Psalm 94:13, argued that, *because it is yet being dug*, there is still time for a change of mind!

> Behold, thou hast the counsel of God, and the reason why he spareth the wicked; the pit is being digged for the sinner. Thou wishest to bury him at once; *the pit is yet being dug for him*: Do not be in haste to bury him' *(Exposition on the Psalms)*.

The message is clear: *Never write anybody off.* Instances of remarkable turnarounds are legion in church history and up to the present time.

Steady patience may also be coupled with what William Wilberforce used to call 'Launchers'. Into a roomful of friends he would deliberately float a question or remark that could be taken up and developed further by another – or dropped, without rancour. Today it might take the form, 'What did you do over the weekend?'

The possibility then arises of the mention of church.

The creation of doubt – by silent example; by a word or Christ-like action, backed up by persevering prayer – here is one of heaven's given ways of reaching some of the most unlikely people who have ever lived.

The part played by relaxed confidence
My saintly missionary mother had returned to England on leave from her pioneer work near Kenya's equator. Later she told me, 'Then one day I received an invitation to meet and hold a detailed discussion with a number of top anthropologists in London who were interested in our area of Kenya. And the topic before us was one in which they were highly erudite.

'Coming up to the building, I was shaking with fear. But then, as I walked into the room and saw these learned professors coming towards me, a shaft of confidence shot through me. I thought to myself, *Not a single one of these men has ever been inside an East African Kikuyu house.'*

It is this principle that we are on about, when representing Jesus Christ in a society embraced by false beliefs. In the first of his New Testament letters, the apostle John writes of false teachers who have gone out into the world. Yet he encourages his Christian readers, when faced by alien worldviews, with these words: 'You, dear children, are from God and have overcome them, because *the one who is in you is greater than the one who is in the world'* (1 John 4:4).

The Spirit of Christ indwells His disciples. He has even bestowed upon us His own delegated authority. We are like the young Malawi police girl of whom I have heard the evangelist Stephen Lungu speak. 'There she will stand,' smiles Stephen, 'a tiny slip of a thing, standing confidently on a lifted pedestal in the centre of our capital city, Lilongwe – white gloves on – with Mercedes, Cadillacs, Land Rovers and great trucks coming towards her. One imperious gesture of her little hand – and, because she has the authority, they all grind to an obedient halt!'

It is never a physical presence that can carry the torch of authority, nor any gifts of intellect or humour. It was a Christian friend of mine, Patrick Sookhdeo, formerly of another religion, who – although he could out-argue his new friends at the London City Mission – was finally obliged to admit to himself, *There is more in these people than there is in me.*

Self-doubt.... Again and again, the path trodden by new believers in Jesus began precisely there.

14

One Link in the Chain

We were at London's All Souls Church one Monday evening, putting on an international diplomatic reception. The hope was that the Christian message might reach some of the Ambassadors and First Secretaries from the many neighbouring embassies. All was ready, and our guest speaker was John Chapman, from Sydney, Australia.

John was in happy, welcoming spirits. Striding up to a tall man in a well-cut dinner suit and bow tie, he extended his hand. 'Good evening, Your Excellency!'

– 'Er, no,' came the rejoinder. 'I'm actually your All Souls drinks waiter!'

John was not deterred. 'Ah, you can't fool me, Your Excellency; I can identify you diplomats a mile off!' Rapidly, I intercepted John, and led him to meet a genuine guest – on his first visit to All Souls. He had come straight from the embassy of what was then still the Soviet Union.

'John,' I announced, 'I'd like you to meet His Excellency Vladimir Demchenko of the Soviet Union!'

A friendly hand reached out from our Australian guest speaker. 'Ullo, Vladimir!' he beamed.

That was the start at church for all of the Demchenko family. And when – after the dismantling of the Soviet Union – the All Souls Orchestra flew to perform in Moscow under the leadership of Noel Tredinnick, who were there to meet us with smiles and hugs but the Demchenkos! It had all begun through an unconsciously disarming handshake from an Australian visitor to London.

A chart of the journey to belief

Os Guinness declares that the journey from non-involvement to full membership in the church of Christ is very rarely completed in a single step, but rather can be traced in a chart of 0 (total non-belief) to full-scale acceptance of Christ, at 100. What figure, then, marked John Chapman's interaction with Vladimir Demchenko? Was he at 5? 32? 70? Only eternity will reveal the answer. In any case, it hardly matters. The Spirit of God uses one and then another in the stages that mark someone's road to faith.

The Scripture stories are many in which an individual was used by heaven as a single link in a chain that led ultimately to the permanent blessing of another. Take the story surrounding a great Syrian general:

> Now Naaman was commander of the army of the king of Aram. He was a great man in the sight of his master.... He was a valiant soldier, but he had leprosy. Now bands from Aram had gone out and had taken captive a young girl from Israel, and she served Naaman's wife. She said to her mistress, 'If only my master would see the prophet who is in Samaria! He would cure him of his leprosy'. (2 Kings 5:1-3)

Naturally, it could be submitted that the part played by Elisha 'the prophet' was notched up somewhere near the 100 mark. It was through him that Naaman accepted the recommended remedy of Jordan's miracle and then finally bowed to the supremacy of the God of Israel. But nothing would have happened without the interposing of the young female prisoner of war – somewhere at the foot of the chart. And at what point were Naaman's faithful servants involved, with their tactful encouragement of their proud master not to refuse the humbling yet saving dip into the despised river waters?

'Operation Andrew'

Then there was Andrew, brother of Simon Peter. He hears John, the Galilean fisherman, referring to Jesus as 'the Lamb of God'. This leads him and a fellow disciple of John to a day spent with Jesus. *'The first thing'* that Andrew then does is to find his brother and inform him, 'We have found the Messiah.' An introduction takes place. (John 1:35-42). It is only later in the story that Peter is eventually inspired to announce before Jesus, 'You are the Christ, Son of the living God!' Yet the opening link had been forged months earlier by Andrew.

The road to personal belief and the links in that chain make a fascinating study. Only a limited selection of examples is open to us, for it is the mysterious – and always unseen – work of the Spirit of God that we are delving into. 'The wind blows wherever it pleases,' explained Jesus. 'You hear its sound, but you cannot tell where it comes from or where it is going. So it is with everyone born of the Spirit' (John 3:8). Yet, ask yourself, How does someone come to faith? How did *you* come to faith?

The surprising chains

History reveals remarkable turnarounds among declared unbelievers, despite the bombastic optimism of their strident champions. In BBC's *Thought for the Day*, the atheist

Richard Dawkins once declared: 'Humanity can now leave the cry-baby stage and learn that it has finally come of age.' Dawkins might have done better to heed the earlier verdict from columnist Bernard Levin: *Those who plan to sit around until it happens to all mankind had better bring a cushion and a very long book* (*The Times*, 16 August 1986).

It only requires a cursory look at the calamitous performances of unleashed modern humanity to explode any theory that the human race can manage on its own. The well-known British philosopher and wartime broadcaster, Professor C.E.M. Joad, had been an agnostic most of his life. He had been in agreement with the theorists who held that evil can be dealt with as a circumstantial problem, relating to environment, lack of education and the growing pains of the human race. But Joad backtracked in 1952 after personal setbacks and the experience of two world wars. In his book, he came to admit that such a theory –

> .... has been rendered utterly unplausible by the events of the last forty years. To me, at any rate, the view of evil implied by Marxism, expressed by Shaw and maintained by modern psychotherapy, a view which regards evil as a by-product of circumstances, which circumstances can therefore alter and even eliminate, has come to seem intolerably shallow. (*Recovery of Belief*, Faber & Faber, 1952)

Don't be surprised

We are predictably surprised by spiritual turnarounds that have taken place, but we should not be. There will be more! Admittedly, few of the supposedly 'great' turn out to be among them. The apostle Paul told the Christian converts at Corinth – '…Think of what you were when you were called. Not many of you were wise by human standards; not many were influential; not many were of noble birth' (1 Cor. 1:26).

To be sure, there have been *some!* It was King Alfred the Great who, through his leadership from the top, left England unmistakably Christian when he died in the year 898. But generally, spiritual revivals tend to start where the common people are – as in the case of the thousands of coal-grimed miners at Kingswood, near Bristol, who weepingly responded to the preaching of George Whitefield in the eighteenth century. We should pray for our politicians and local leaders by all means, but widespread spiritual transformation never originated with them. It is when the grassroots produce chains of personal belief on a wide scale that society at large can change. And even the most surprising chains can be forged through the feeblest of links!

The weakest links

For the apostle Paul had gone on to assure his protégés at Corinth:

> But God chose the foolish things of the world to shame the wise; God chose the weak things of the world to shame the strong. He chose the lowly things of this world and the despised things – and the things that are not – to nullify the things that are, so that no-one may boast before him. (1 Cor. 1:27-29)

Indeed the whole of Paul's correspondence with the Corinthians can be summed up under the theme *Power through Weakness*. Dick Lucas, of St Helen's Church in London's Bishopsgate, once said, 'When you see the power of God at work, what you see is weakness.'

Moscow again

The stories for our encouragement are legion. On our – related earlier – orchestral visit to Moscow Noel Tredinnick and I found inspiration through Oleg, our Russian interpreter. 'I suppose you were brought up in a Christian family,' I hazarded.

– 'Not at all!' was the reply. 'I grew up as an atheist and joined the Young Communist League. But in the school where I taught, the Head came to me one day, and said, "I want you to go and sort out a problem pupil we have. She's going around saying that she's a Christian. Worse still, she's a Baptist!"

'My first surprise, when I got to her', continued Oleg, 'was that she was only seven years of age! My second surprise came when she replied to my remonstration, with her first question to me, *"How sure* are you that there is no God?"

'I had to admit that I wasn't 100 per cent certain of my position…. and sensing my indecision, she worked her way into my defences, and led me to faith in Jesus Christ that very day. *It was the most embarrassing moment of my life!'*

Naturally, we had to have Oleg visit us later, back in London.

How a missionary was produced

God used a weeping child coming out of Sunday School one day in London. A woman saw her in the street, and bent over to comfort her.

– 'No, I'm not sad,' declared the girl. 'But I've heard wonderful things about God today, and I'm so happy I can't stop crying!'

– 'But…. that's what I want!' declared the adult. 'Where did you hear this?'

– 'Just over there', pointed the girl. 'If you go to that hall, they'll tell you!'

And that very thing happened. A vital link was forged that afternoon, and the time came when the now-believing woman was interviewed by my mother for Christian service overseas. The little girl never knew that in her earliest moments of Christian joy she had been used in the providence of God to produce a missionary.

The Overseas Missionary Fellowship once reported the story of a religious procession featuring a holy man atop an elephant. A humble, dispirited colporteur below was distributing Christian tracts.... and the grey trunk, that was collecting gifts from every side, descended his way, came down, took the tract and carried it above. It was later that the holy man confessed that, on reading the pamphlet, he came to the realisation that he was not holy at all, and needed the very forgiveness of Christ in his life.

Links in a chain! We may not ourselves be able to analyse every element, big or small, that has operated in our own story – and for a good reason....

The anonymous Spirit

There is a strange and deliberate anonymity about the working of the Spirit of God. He points, not to Himself, but rather to Christ. **His role within the Trinity is to make Christ real to people.** He works unseen as the wind. It was He who guided Philip, the evangelist, to speak with an Ethiopian treasury official who was on the road to Gaza. *The Spirit told Philip, 'Go to that chariot, and stay near it'* (Acts 8:29). Philip, then, was a willing link in the adventure that took Christianity into North Africa.

Hey, He can use you, parent, today – at the school gate! My wife Pam once spoke with another mother, while collecting her boy at the end of lessons. 'I wasn't even trying', remembers Pam, 'but Lesley and I got talking and somehow the opportunity presented itself when I later plucked up courage to buy her a Bible. Lesley was eventually to tell me "You'll never know what that meant to me". Later

I learnt that it was a relation of mine who was the prayer link behind all that was happening.'

One link in the chain. The newest followers of Christ may ask to be filled with the Holy Spirit every morning, as heads rise from the pillow. *Who shall I be meeting today.... at the workplace....on the campus.... down the road ? How can I please my Lord? Let me walk at His side, as an ambassador of truth and love.*

15

'Doesn't it Say Somewhere...?'

Over many years I have developed a habit, when leading a congregation in church, of inviting everyone to learn some key verse of Scripture with me. Generally this happens spontaneously – if I sense that the proceedings are becoming a little too predictable.

The reference first. Then the sentence itself. Then the reference once again. *That way, you can drive it in.* 'Test each other over coffee afterwards!' I urge.

Pauline Wenn, mother of a young family, felt irritated, the first time she heard me lead such an exercise. *It was a bit like going back to school,* she told me later. Yet, dramatic repercussions resulted. On the very next day, Pauline found herself chatting with her near neighbour, Olive Burchell.

'There's something you have from that church of yours that I haven't got!' exclaimed Olive, 'and I want you to tell me how I can have it too.'

– 'Well, I'll be glad to talk with you about it some time,' replied Pauline.

– 'No, I want to know now. Come on!'

Pauline began to flounder. As she told me later: 'I'd never tried to explain the Christian life to anyone else. I didn't know where to start. *"Wow,"* I thought, *"this is terrible. I know so little. And I don't know a single verse of the Bi – Yes I do.... I learnt it in church last night!"'* And out it came:

> For it is by grace you have been saved, through faith – and this not from yourselves, it is the gift of God – not by works, so that no one can boast.' (Eph. 2:8-9)

The two chatted on. There was enough in Ephesians 2:8 and 9 for Olive to receive the free grace of God in Jesus Christ that very day. She joined the church and went on to become a trusted leader.

Ephesians 2:8 and 9! Here is the identical Scripture that had first led J.C. Ryle, the first Bishop of Liverpool, into faith before he exercised his mighty writing and preaching gifts in the nineteenth century.

Learn memory verses! Ignore the well-tried excuses: *I've got a useless memory for anything.... There are so many Bible versions these days.... People don't want 'proof' texts' shoved down their throats.... I'm a bit too old now to start learning verses by heart....*

Little by little, however slowly, we can rid ourselves of the tendency to find ourselves muttering, 'But doesn't it say somewhere....?'

Even if it takes a lifetime!

We owe it to our members

Calling church leaders, ministers, class teachers, bishops! We owe it to our members to get portions of Scripture into the thinking of the entire fellowship. True, it will be an advantage if someone memorising the words of Jesus in Mark 10:45 can also place it correctly in the wider surrounding of the disciples' controversy with James and

John about servanthood. *But even the text itself gives the memoriser a vital handle to work with.*

I once led our congregation in memorising together a scrap from Hebrews 9:27 with its statement that ... *man is destined to die once, and after that to face judgment....* A visiting American present learnt it and later wrote to us in London from the U.S.A., to testify to the value of this Bible sentence in a conversation with a friend who till then had believed in the 'many' successive lives of Reincarnation teaching.

We owe it to friends of other beliefs

Have you ever been told by a member of another belief-system that nowhere in the Christian Scriptures is it ever stated specifically that it was the shedding of the blood of Jesus that provided the forgiveness of people's sins? Were we able to bring the words of Jesus Himself, in Matthew 26:28, to their attention? Or what about Revelation 1:17 and 18, as an answer to the charge that nowhere does Jesus declare for *Himself* that – though He was dead – He is now alive for ever? Or what of the claim that has been commonly made that no reference can be found to the Ascension of Jesus *specifically up to heaven?* In quiet moments, I review such references as Luke 9:51, Luke 24:51, Acts 1:11, 1 Peter 3:22.... ready for the next time! As Dawson Trotman, of The Navigators Association – and then his successor Lorne Sanny – used to say, *Review, review, review!*

A fellowship of Assent

Naturally, nothing can replace the supreme importance of what is gained from entire Scripture passages, whether in public expository preaching, group work or personal study. But a congregation also establishes its distinctive identity as a 'Bible people' from the added-value of a single

Scripture sentence – memorised together, *and led from the front.* Such a simple exercise helps to pinpoint the fact that we are deliberately becoming 'a fellowship of assent' to the truth of the holy Scriptures that are able to make us wise for salvation through faith in Christ Jesus (2 Tim. 3:15).

This is a cumulative exercise. The journey of a thousand memory verses begins with a single text! My first-ever was from the King James Version: *'Philippians 4:4: – Rejoice in the Lord always: and again I say, Rejoice.... Philippians 4: 4.'* Memorising can become a highly fulfilling and regular activity – as a particular sentence from our daily reading seems to glow and interject itself upon our memory. We go out into the day with it. On the Underground or Metro we review it. At bedtime we murmur it once more. Reference.... Text.... Reference again! In our subconscious, there is a fair chance that it will stay with us all night.

The world of suffering

True, it is not simply the glib rattling out of a single text of Scripture that is going to satisfy our own deep questions, let alone those of our unchurched friends. You do not blandly trot out Romans 8:28 (*All things work together for good....*) in the face of a neighbour's anguished bereavement. And what of Pompeii in A.D. 79, or 'The Black Death' of the fourteenth century – that killed 20 million people between Iceland and India? As the French chronicler Jean Froissart wrote, 'A third of the world died.'

The hurricanes, tsunamis and earthquakes; the elimination of six million Jews in World War II; the ethnic cleansings, children's slave trafficking and religious-inspired atrocities are all drawn into today's debates.

It was this very need to try to address these and other issues that prompted me to write my book, *The Top 100 Questions* (Christian Focus Publications). It was a modest attempt on my part to face questions asked of me by both Christians and the unchurched across many years. I grouped the answers under the five headings of The Universe We Inhabit, The Truth We Believe, The Bible We Read, The Way We Behave and The Christ We Follow.

Perhaps the 'top' blockbuster of all time is that which questions the existence of a God of love in a world of suffering. C.S. Lewis wrestled with it valiantly in his book *The Problem of Pain* (HarperCollins). In more recent years, Bishop Michael Baughen's magnificent book *The One Big Question* (CWR, 2010) was praised in a foreword by Archbishop George Carey for 'facing head-on this most intractable of problems'.

Ethical questions around the beginning and end of human life continually arise on our television screens. They include euthanasia, abortion, infanticide, disability, cloning and the new genetics, the use of embryos for research, and plenty more. Professor John Wyatt – who is frequently asked for television interviews – brilliantly takes up these modern issues from a biblical standpoint in his highly researched, yet readable book *Matters of Life and Death* (InterVarsity Press).

In facing a world of militant atheism that is out to destroy the Christian faith, we will get to know writers such as John Lennox, David Robertson, Michael Nazir-Ali, Chris Wright and Ravi Zacharias – who are well known for their brilliant, God-given gifts in out-arguing atheism's top advocates.

Building up your own library

The modern Christian, then, needs to face the question, *How is your library growing?* Whether your library is of books on a shelf or books downloaded electronically as ebooks in such well-known readers as *Kindle*, we need steadily to be building up our own library of favoured books by trusted authors. (TIP: 'Know your reviewer'). Biblically inspired books are going to help us negotiate the rocks and currents of modern issues.

Books! They can change people's lives and in doing so can change the world. Guy King has written:

'Richard Sibbes, an old Puritan, wrote a little book called *The Bruised Reed.* One day it fell into the hands of a tin pedlar, who gave it to a boy called Richard Baxter, who, through reading it, became in time the saintly Richard Baxter of Kidderminster. In process of time Baxter wrote *A Call to the Unconverted,* and by doing so kindled the flame in the heart of Philip Doddridge, who in turn wrote a book called *The Rise and Progress of Religion in the Soul.*

'This fell into the hands of William Wilberforce, changed his life, and led the great emancipator of the slaves to write *A Practical View of Christianity.* By reading this, the heart of Leigh Richmond underwent a strange blossoming, and, as one result, he wrote *The Dairyman's Daughter,* which besides being the most powerful religious influence in the life of Queen Victoria, had a good deal to do with the transformation of Thomas Chalmers, who in his turn touched the whole world' (*To My Son,* CLC Publications).

The right book in the right hand

Calling church leaders, ministers, class leaders, bishops! Put in charge of your fellowship or church bookstall someone responsible enough to select such books as will accord with *the great Bible emphases demanded of faithful ministry for Jesus Christ.* We are not to be duped by those who advocate 'other books' with diversionist leanings – on the grounds that 'our members need a broad understanding of all religious outlooks in the church.' That approach leads to utter confusion. **In any case, our members are bound to be introduced to those**

'other books' from many different quarters, whether they wish it or not. The right book in the right hand at the right moment was what led Queen Candace's chancellor to discover Christ and take the Christian message into Ethiopia.

We need Bible 'tools' such as commentaries, Bible handbooks and reference books; different Bible versions, Christian biographies and books on doctrine; books on church history, on discipleship and Christian service – and books that might be described simply as 'thrillmanship.' Little by little, the Christian worker becomes 'prepared to give an answer to everyone who asks you to give the reason for the hope that you have' (1 Pet. 3:15).

We can turn to a book from some Old Testament prophet, written several hundred years before the birth of Christ – and discover that what was then little more than a pamphlet-sized tract for a Middle East nomadic society contains timeless truth that addresses itself to questions raised by citizens of the twenty-first century, ranging from Beijing to Belfast.

With the Bible, we start far ahead of others as we, in our turn, grapple with the very same searing questions that faced Job, Habakkuk or Jonah long ago. An outsider to the Christian faith will never get close to even the glimmering of an answer to some of the deeper questions of life and eternity, or personal significance. We find some of these questions hard enough ourselves! But it is infinitely harder for the non-believer. At the very least, these big issues involving our existence and the meaning of life *are themselves built into – and are an integral part of – our biblical worldview.* We are given handles that we can work with; handles that the Marxists of old or today's agnostic has no recourse to whatever.

'Doesn't it say somewhere?....' Yes it does!

Part Four:

The Authentic Lifestyle

How was it done? Here we touch what I think is one of the greatest wonders that history has to show. How did the Church do it? If I may invent or adapt three words, the Christian 'out-lived' the pagan, 'out-died' him and 'out-thought' him.

T.R. GLOVER
The Jesus of History, SCM, 1917, p. 213

16

The Worker's Personal Life

Have you been given a Bible study group to look after? You can feel both exhilarated and shaky when a thing like this happens. I can remember in my early twenties being asked to lead a party of boys in England's Lake District. Half of them had been in trouble with the police and were on probation. It was a marvellous yet terrifying responsibility.

My own missionary father once took on the building of a church, in East Africa; till then he had never built anything more than a chicken coop.

New assignments can raise in us a mixed sense of privilege and fear. But what must it have been like when Titus, the Greek-born 'partner and fellow-worker' of the apostle Paul, was given an entire island to look after, around A.D. 60?

> .... I left you in Crete.... that you might straighten out what was left unfinished and appoint elders in every town, as I directed you.... (Titus 1:5)

In every town? Several centuries earlier, the Greek poet Homer had declared that Crete – a sizeable island dominating the south of the Aegean Sea – had as many as a hundred towns and cities. The task set before Titus, then, was daunting. My son Stephen and his family have enjoyed regular summer breaks in Crete, and I have witnessed for myself its mountainous and formidable terrain. It had known violent times when overrun by pirates around 1400 B.C. By the time of Titus, Crete had been a part of the Roman empire for nearly a century, but it was never an easy walkover for any intruders.

Who wants the task?

To be sure, there had been Cretans at Pentecost (Acts 2:11), and it seems the church in Crete would have been born then. At some unknown point, Paul's first visit to the island took place, and now – following his imprisonment in Rome – he had handed the island over to Titus, to carry on the work of the gospel. But superstition was rife; Crete was supposedly the birthplace of Zeus. Bacchus, the god of the grape harvest and of wine, was worshipped there. Who would want to take on the task of 'straightening out' a shaky and disordered church in such an environment?

But this has been a regular occurrence. I can think of faithful servants of Jesus Christ who will willingly accept a call to a remote mission outpost, a slum area, a parish that in living memory has never heard the Bible faithfully proclaimed – and make it the business of their life to turn it into gold.

Wisdom and modesty

Historical observation seems to confirm the teaching of Scripture that – when the dust has finally settled – those whom posterity honours are the individuals recognised for the wisdom and modesty of their living. Plutarch, the Greek philosopher of the fourth century B.C., said that when young men came to study in Athens, they were 'wise men'; after they had studied a little, they were only 'lovers of wisdom' – and at the end of their course described themselves as 'fools'.

Even more so is the quality of humble integrity required in a servant of Jesus Christ! The letters to Timothy and Titus have been widely hailed as 'The Pastoral Letters', and are vital reading for anyone active in God's service. The Puritan leader of old, Thomas Manton, highlighted this requirement:

> O ye ministers of the Word, consider well that you are the first sheets from the King's (printing) press; others are printed after your copy. If the first sheet be well set, a thousand more are stamped with ease. See, then, that the power of religion prevail over your own hearts, lest you lose not only your own souls, but cause the ruin of others. *(England's Spiritual Languishing; its Causes and Cure)*

This was to be the burning concern for Titus. He was to model gospel living, in the 'straightening' of his fellow leaders in Crete. On the personal level, several qualities emerge in Paul's letter to Titus:

God's servant is to be blameless in public

> 'An elder must be blameless, the husband of but one wife, a man whose children believe and are not open to the charge of being wild and disobedient. Since an overseer is entrusted with God's work, he must be blameless – not overbearing, not quick-tempered, not given to drunkenness, not violent, not pursuing dishonest gain.' (Titus 1:6, 7)

'Blameless'…. The word occurs twice, but be comforted that the word is not 'flawless'! *Blameless* implies that true servants of the gospel – with all their faults and mannerisms – should nevertheless be seen to be in good standing within their society. A passage like Titus 1: 6-9 (or its parallel in 1 Timothy 3:1-13) should be read publicly before the appointment or election of officers takes place in a fellowship, for it is vital that no breath or whisper of moral scandals among us should bring shame to Christ's face.

In the Sermon on the Mount, Jesus exhorted His listeners to blameless living. 'Be perfect,' he declared, 'as your heavenly Father is perfect.' That is the standard, and we are to aim at it! Is 99 per cent permissible, we might ask? No! Francis Schaeffer once wrote, 'How could a perfect God say, "Just sin a little bit!"' (*The God Who is There*, IVP, page 155).

The challenging of the culture

Standards are slipping today across the whole of the West, and it is up to the church *not to adapt itself to the surrounding culture but rather to stand up and challenge it.* This is exactly what the early Christians were inspired to do, in their bold witness to a Greek and Roman society that was infinitely more gross than anything we know today.... *and steadily they succeeded.*

Naturally, our critics have derided us all down history for our attempt to uphold and preach Christ's standards. The second-century Roman philosopher Celsus scoffed at the Christians of his time for their challenge to the morality of the day when, for example, they upheld marriage, offering cleansing and new power in Christ's name. Celsus flatly disbelieved that Christianity could achieve a change in lifestyle for anybody – and the Stoic thinkers agreed with him.

But then came the great surprise. 'The Christians', wrote the historian T.R. Glover, 'came with a message of the highest conceivable morality.... They expected a response;

they preached repentance and reformation, and people did respond; they repented and they lived new lives' (*The Influence of Christ in the Ancient World*, Cambridge University Press, 1933, page 75).

But there's more. If the Cretan leaders needed the call to blamelessness in public, their private living also needed attention:

God's servant is to be controlled in private

Are there figures in church leadership today who deserve this description of some of those whom Titus was to 'straighten out'?

> Even one of their own prophets has said, 'Cretans are always liars, evil brutes, lazy gluttons.' This testimony is true. Therefore, rebuke them sharply, so that they will be sound in the faith.... To the pure, all things are pure, but to those who are corrupted and do not believe, nothing is pure. (Titus 1:12, 13, 15)

In quoting from Epimenides – the Cretans' own prophet of the sixth century B.C. – Paul is not attacking Titus' flock with an age-old ethnic stereotype. Rather, this ancient epitaph from their own history was being used to illustrate how ungodliness can penetrate any culture, including their own – and even cause the church's leadership to run in a deviationist direction, and behave as *liars, evil brutes* and *lazy gluttons*.

This has happened today in the warped leadership of certain church circles in today's Western world. Members of the top hierarchy have been known to change the locks on local churches that they plan to usurp. They have hacked into the computers of faithful gospel ministers and had them ejected from their calling. They have lied, cheated, sued and bribed in their attempt at personal validation and power. The words of the New Testament here apply not simply to the false teachers in Crete, but directly to these of the twenty-first century who have deserted the faith and behave worse than the unchurched. Paul's words are apt here, when he writes, *'They claim to know God, but by their actions they deny him. They are detestable, disobedient and unfit for doing anything good'* (Titus 1:16).

The Bible's searchlight falls upon us all! How are we doing in the control of our life, our study and service – *on the private front?*

We are called to be disciplined

'Controlled' is a key word in the letter to Titus. The 'over-seer' is to be *self-controlled* (1:8) and so are the 'older men' (2:2), the 'younger women' (2:5), the 'young men' (2:6) and indeed all who embrace God's salvation (2:12).

It seems that all who ever rose to effectiveness in the public service of God knew something of this priority. **If we want to be effective for Jesus, we must spend *time* with Jesus!** Our whole day needs to come under His control. It is this observance of discipline that surely explains how it is that in Christian work the busiest people (and even the untidy ones!) always seem to have time for everything and everyone! Think of John Wesley, who rode the equivalent of ten times round the world on horseback and preached forty thousand sermons. Read his words:

> Whenever I see one or a thousand men running into hell, be it in England, Ireland or France; yea, in Europe, Asia, Africa or America, I will stop them if I can. But though I am always in haste, I am never in a hurry; because I never undertake any more work than I can go through with per-fect calmness of spirit. *(Letter to John Smith of Dublin, 1747)*

Blameless.... Controlled – but how do we come across to others?

God's servant is to be consistent in practice

What you see is what you get! There is to be no cover-up, no hypocritical show. There is a wholesomeness about the man or woman whose apparent shining exterior is equally as winsome when behind closed doors. 'To the pure,' Paul had written, 'all things are pure, but to those who are corrupted and do not believe, nothing is pure' (Titus 1:15).

The point is made that the pure in heart will leave the touch of purity *upon everything they do.* Equally, if corruption has a hold upon the citadel of somebody's soul, *everything they touch will be tainted.* Christians of every age – even the slaves of the first century – had it in them, by their style of service, to make the truth of Christ 'attractive' (Titus 2:9, 10). We are to give the picture of Christ's love a suitable frame, yet in full recognition that the frame is not there to draw attention to itself!

A glowing tribute

And this was the role of Titus. A regular travelling companion of Paul, he is wonderfully described with others as 'representatives of the churches and an honour to Christ' (2 Cor. 8:23). **Whenever Titus showed up, the sun shone.** Under intense harassment, Paul wrote, 'But God, who comforts the downcast, comforted us by the coming of Titus' (2 Cor. 7:6).

It is possible, it seems, to achieve prominence in God's service – yet always to stay at the feet of Christ. This was apparent in the life of the modest gospel singer, George Beverly Shea, who departed this world in the spring of 2013, aged 104. During more than sixty years, he visited some 148 countries with the evangelist Billy Graham. Despite Grammy awards – and his world record of singing to more people than any other artist in history, secular or religious – *it never got to him.* For him it was not Crete, but rather a lifetime of singing for God…. and he accepted it. In *Decision* magazine, April 1989, he commented, 'I suggest to young people, *Don't put your hand on the knob to open the door. Let God do it. He will!*

17

'Give Me This Mountain!'

When it comes to the future vision of the Christian, here are two pieces of contrasting advice given by equally godly and wise Christian leaders. One – featured in our previous chapter – was offered by the gospel singer, George Beverly Shea:

> 'Don't put your hand on the knob to open the door. Let God do it. He will!'

The other was given by Fred Mitchell, former international missionary statesman and chairman of the Keswick Convention, held annually in England's Lake District:

> 'The door of opportunity is marked *Push*.'

We need not think the two pieces of advice cancel each other out. Both attitudes are entwined around each other as part of a single, shared vision and long-established desire *that it must be God who is writing the script*. Thus it happened one day that George Beverly Shea was walking down London's Regent Street, when he chanced to meet an old friend – and was handed an obscure song of Russian origin, entitled 'How Great Thou Art.' Eventually, he felt inspired to use it in every meeting without fail, during sixteen weeks of nightly preaching by Billy Graham in New York's Madison Square Garden – and thus gave the song a decisive push.... around the whole world.

And Fred Mitchell was a stocky Yorkshire businessman who developed an overwhelming desire to push out and reach China for the gospel. Despite his desires, the way seemed constantly blocked by circumstances. 'When I am dead,' he had said, 'you will find China written on my heart.' For years he was obliged to wait. He continued with his work in pharmacy, meanwhile establishing prayer meetings in his spare time and joining the council of the China Inland Mission. Then one day the long wait ended, when an unexpected letter arrived, inviting him to take over the directorship of the entire mission. Suddenly, China was *on*.

Whatever the style and approach to God's service – and however great the frustrations and delays – the vital underlying motivation of any servant of God must be that expressed by the Psalmist: 'I delight to do thy will, O my God' (Ps. 40:8, KJV).

The interests of the kingdom

'Seek ye first the kingdom of God, and his righteousness; and all these things shall be added unto you' (Matt. 6:33 KJV). Interpreting these words of Jesus, Bishop Alf Stanway, of Melbourne, made the point that ministers for God can do one of two things. Either they may do everything possible to look after their own interests – and God will let them do so. Alternatively, they can bend their chief energies towards looking after the interests of the kingdom of God.... and God will look after their interests. 'In all of my ministry over the years,' said Alf, 'I have proved that the second approach is the preferable.'

Ambition – or *Vision*? 'Ambition' all too often bears a worldly, self-promoting connotation. Perhaps 'Vision' better describes the Christian worker who, in daily life and work, is fired ultimately by the advance, worldwide, of the kingdom of God. Even the Christian slaves of Paul's time (there were sixty million slaves in the Roman empire) were taken as a model of how this could be done, by pleasing their masters and to refrain from theft.

The Christian revolution

Would it not have been more revolutionary to defy the Roman system and throw off their shackles – in the name of God's kingdom? The answer was No. Such a response would have been to reduce Christ to the level of a mere Spartacus or a Che Guevara. Within the Christian fellowship itself Christ's followers did something more revolutionary still – by simply ignoring the master-slave relationship altogether and treating one another 'no longer as a slave, but better than a slave, as a dear brother' (Philem. 16). This attitude would slowly drip-feed its way through society, until the empire itself collapsed.

But let us take an example from the Bible, neither of a slave, nor of an important personage, but of an *Average Person* from thirty-three centuries ago – namely Caleb. Caleb had never had any official position of leadership in Israel. He was simply a member of the tribe of Judah. Nothing much characterised this 'average man,' beyond one vital – and repeated – description, and that was that 'he followed the Lord wholeheartedly.' If any man or woman can be so described, nothing else really matters.

'Give me this mountain'

And Caleb was of pensionable age when he came into his own, with a call to Joshua for his rightful claim in the

Promised Land as it came into view: 'Give me this mountain' (Josh. 14:12, KJV). Caleb's active days had been forty-five years earlier, when he had been one of a number of Israelite spies, sent to do a feasibility study on a takeover of Canaan, the Promised Land. At that time his positive assessment to 'Go forward' had been sidelined as a minority report, and only Joshua himself had lined up with him. Now, as a man of eighty-five, active life was apparently 'over'.

And if we ask what, today, in Christian terms, is represented by 'The Promised Land', the answer is *All that is included in the word 'Salvation'*; that is – forgiveness of sins, new life by the Spirit of God, membership of God's church and His eternal kingdom; increasing domination over all that pulls us back from holiness of living… together with that ultimate share in the future New Heaven and New Earth at the end of the world, when Christ returns. Indeed, some of it still lies ahead for the believer.

At this time, the Israelites, under Joshua, were still entering into the benefits of their 'salvation' – God's rescue of them from oppression in Egypt, under Moses' leadership, years earlier; they had then spent years in the wilderness, as they headed towards their Promised Land; there had been many battles and there was still plenty that they had to work out. Moses was dead, and the new leader, Joshua, began to try to parcel out fairly – among the tribes of Israel – the land that they had so far occupied.

The enduring vision

Enter Caleb, of the tribe of Judah, once again! He is wanting something out of his leader Joshua. He is looking at the tough, violent terrain of Hebron and he says, *'Give me this mountain.'* 'What?' we think. 'At that time of life?' What prompted Caleb to ask for this at a time when we would think he was ready to bow out of the scene?

Yet down the years Caleb had held on to a pledge made to him by Moses those forty-five years earlier – and that vision had stayed in his mind throughout the time of the wilderness. He now reminds Joshua of their joint minority report as spies, and of Moses' determination, years earlier, to reward them for their bold recommendations. This is how Caleb had phrased that early report:

> Only rebel not ye against the Lord, neither fear ye the people of the land, for they are bread for us; their defence is departed from them, and the Lord is with us; fear them not. (Num. 14:9 kjv)

They'll be bread for us. 'No contest!' had been Caleb's buoyant utterance. Caleb now stakes his claim: *Joshua, remember that day and that promise? Give me this mountain!*

Taking on the roughest

The old promise was what energised Caleb for his successful, late-life adventure, and we have only to look up Deuteronomy 1:35 and 36, to discover further that the promise to Caleb had originally been *God's* promise. Caleb now takes on the roughest and most challenging piece of land available, mountainous Hebron.

The real operators for God are so often the ones who opt for the hardest assignments! We can contrast Caleb's mindset with that of the tribes of Ephraim and Manasseh. They could only complain. '*Why*', they asked, 'have you given us only one allotment and one portion for an inheritance? We are a numerous people, and the Lord has blessed us abundantly' (Josh. 17:14).

Joshua challenges them: 'If you are so numerous, and if the hill country of Ephraim is too small for you, go up into the forest and clear land for yourselves there in the land of the Perizzites and Rephaites' (Josh. 17:15)

But no, they can't accept that. They see the iron chariots of the Canaanite people (v. 16), and they draw back, even though they have more resources than Caleb – whereas Caleb, for his part, is content to take on three mighty Anakite generals (Josh. 15:14). And then he will take on *HEBRON*.

The front-liners

And that, broadly, is the difference between the front-liner and the back-liner in life with God. If you had gone to the front line when Israel was locked in battle, and asked, 'How are you getting on?' the reply would have been, 'Well, we're managing! We've lost a quarter of our men in the last hour, and if you could send up some more bows and arrows, that would help. But we can hold this hill; we'll cope!'

Then you go to the back line. 'What's happening here?' – 'Oh, it's terrible. The food's awful. And... my tent leaks!' *That is the difference.* We find it today in much of church life.

Who are the front-liners, the Calebs of today? I think of a Middle-East Christian leader who – at a time of severe instability and conflict within his own country – set up a new church. 'Wasn't that a very difficult moment – to begin a new church?' I asked him. 'No,' he smiled, 'it was the *best* moment!'

'I'll take Hebron – Give me this mountain!' Nothing can stand in the way of such people. Caleb 'wholeheartedly' followed the Lord. In the Hebrew text, the word 'wholehearted' conveys the idea of a ship under full sail.

On to the next adventure

We, today, can reach a point when we are relying on money, publicity, oratory or good connections, and think that the power lies there! It never did. God says, 'The spirit of *Caleb* is the one I can use – and bless!'.... Such a man or woman, of whatever age, is spiritually young; reaching out always for the next adventure, who says in prayer, *Give me this mountain!*

D. L. Moody, of Chicago, 150 years ago was a Sunday School leader. 'Give me this Sunday School!' was his prayer. God blessed him and his ministry expanded. 'Give me Chicago!' he prayed, and before long, all Chicago was at Moody's feet; people found the Lord wherever he preached in that great city. 'Give me the world!' prayed Moody, and his ministry became mountainous. It is said that Moody put one hand on America and the other on Britain, and lifted both those two countries heavenwards – winning millions of people to Christ in the process.

Caleb now was eighty-five years old. Physically, he was not what he had been, but spiritually he was a <u>force</u>! Michael Baughen, my predecessor in central London, undertook a massive building extension at All Souls Church. He declared that there were three stages when you are faced as a Christian worker with an unassailable mountain: *Impossible – difficult – DONE!*

'Give me this mountain!' Could that be our own prayer this very day?

> God, give me that Sunday School to lead!
> Give me that position at my workplace and I'll make it productive for your glory!
> Give me those neighbours in my street! I covet them for Your kingdom!
> Give me that one person I've been praying for.
> Give me those members of my family!
> Give me that church to look after for You!

And those of us who preach and teach in the villages and cities of this world; why, we may find ourselves praying: *Give me... Tonbridge in Kent! Give us... Aberdeen in Scotland! Give us Buenos Aires... Nairobi... Manhattan... Sydney!*

And when we reach up in prayer like this, it may be that something of the spirit of Caleb of old will come up to you, and you'll hear a faint whisper in your ear, 'Don't worry; it'll be all right....'

'They'll be bread for you.'

18

Don't Block
the Blessing!

There is a seventeenth-century painting by Rubens, of
Thetis – the mother of Achilles in Greek mythology – dip-
ping her son into the supposedly protective waters of the
river Styx. But, because she held him by his heel, this single
part of him was untouched by the water. Achilles grew to
be a mighty warrior; yet, during a fateful battle, an arrow
that pierced his vulnerable heel was the means of his downfall.

The Achilles heel has come to represent that fragile part
of even the most powerful and virtuous.

An old fable relates how the Devil was once crossing the
Libyan desert, and came upon a group of junior devils who
were tempting a holy hermit. They tried him with seductions of the flesh; they inserted doubts into his mind; they
told him that all his discipline was a waste of time. But all
was useless – the holy man stayed holy.

The Devil then stepped forward and intervened.

– 'Your methods are so crude, so ham-fisted! Permit me!'

Going up to the hermit, he said, 'Have you heard the good
news? Your brother has been made Bishop of Alexandria!'

It was only then that the face of the holy man began to twist and contort with jealousy and hurt pride.

Even the strongest can fail

That Achilles-heel factor affects every single one of us. Indeed, some of the prominent Bible characters were brought down not even at their weakest point but at their strongest. We have only to read of faithful Noah, who – soon after the triumph of the Flood and the establishing of the Covenant with God – is found blind drunk. There was David, the human archetype of love, who, following his victory over the Ammonites, falls in love with Bathsheba, commits adultery and then engineers the death of her husband, Uriah.

This is the warning to every servant of God. My own mother testified to this common experience among Christian workers:

> 'You return on the train, from a brilliant and inspiring time of mission in a university. You've been praying and working hard – and seeing God at work. Now you're elated – and at last relaxed. This is the exact moment when you are off your guard. It is then that the Devil strikes – in one way or another – to bring you down.'

This was the sequence of events when Jesus was baptised – at the high moment of His baptism; when heaven was opened, when the Spirit descended like a dove and the Voice was heard, 'This is my Son, whom I love; with him I am well pleased.' Immediately there followed the temptation in the wilderness: '*If you are the Son of God*, tell these stones to become bread.'

Staying on guard

We can follow the example of our Leader, who was 'tempted in every way, just as we are – yet was without sin' (Heb. 4:15)

– and learn to stay on guard. It is the maintaining of our daily union with Jesus that keeps our service intact and pure.

For, once we are joined to Christ by faith, His destiny becomes our destiny! To quote from my colleague Paul Blackham, our relationship with Him from then on will be like that of a needle with its thread. *Wherever the needle goes, the attached thread follows.* Thus it is that our own destiny is wrapped up in Christ's. It is rewarding to observe the four instances in a New Testament passage, where Paul's Christian readers were said to be 'with Christ':

> Since you **died with Christ** to the basic principles of this world, why, as though you still belonged to it, do you submit to its rules: 'Do not handle! Do not taste! Do not touch!'?...... Since, then, you have been **raised with Christ**, set your hearts on things above, where Christ is seated at the right hand of God. Set your minds on things above, not on earthly things. For you died, and your life is now **hidden with Christ** in God. When Christ, who is your life, appears, then you also will **appear with him** in glory. (Col. 2:20, 21; 3:1-4)

Four great stages

Here are four great stages of our salvation, all of them concerned with Christ and the salvation that He brings. He *died* for the sins of the world. He was *raised* on that third momentous day. He ascended to heaven forty days later – there to be *hidden* from the world's view. Finally, He will be *appearing* at the end of the world, in final judgment, and to usher in the new heaven and the new earth. And every believer is threaded inexorably into all four stages.

He died – to take upon Himself the judgment that would otherwise have banished us for ever from the presence of God.... and His death means that we have 'died,' in that we are no longer accountable at the judgment; we can be said to have died *with Christ*. Further, **Jesus was raised**, historically and bodily from the grave. Because His followers are tied to Him ever since they came into union with Him by faith, they are assured that they have been raised with Him. *'Have been* raised'.... That is the language used! True, a resurrection body, like His – free from decay and pain – still lies in the future, but the assurance is that the life of Christ's resurrection is at work in the believer in the immediate present! Once joined to Christ, our resurrection life is already under way. Here and now, we are children of eternity.... so we are to *live* like children of the resurrection!

Hidden, safe and secure

Take it further. Jesus ascended to heaven – there to **be hidden** from the eyes of the world, as He exercises His triumphant rule. We too, because we are united with Him, are also said to be hidden with Him. To the outward eye, we can be seen, walking, eating, working.... but there is a part of us that is hidden from the world's gaze. My wife Pam describes it as 'Otherness'. Sometimes we become aware of this unfathomable element of something 'extra' about a Christian man or woman, whose spirit is joined in intimacy to that of Jesus. Where Christ is, no one can touch or harm Him; so it has been with thousands of witnesses and martyrs who have staked all on the conviction that their real selves are hidden, safe and secure for ever with their unseen Companion.

And the fourth 'episode'? It still lies ahead – on that Day when the kingdoms of this world will become the kingdom of our Lord and of His Christ (Rev. 11:15). It will be the Day of 'the glorious appearing of our great God and Saviour, Jesus Christ (Titus 2:13). Believe it, Christian! Whether you are a disciple of many years, or have received

Christ just days ago, this will be your inheritance – that you will be appearing with Him on that Day.

His destiny – my destiny

All four 'episodes' follow each other and belong together. We cannot separate them into different compartments. It would be ridiculous for a believer to assert, 'Well, I have died with Christ; my sins have been judged in His death for me – but I cannot yet say that I am hidden in Him.' No. All four of these salvation verbs flow together as Christ's great saving embrace of His believing people. If I am united with Him, then He will take me with Him, as day follows night, as the thread follows the needle. *I'm attached....* His destiny is my destiny!

However, if massive blessings belong to those in union with Christ, it follows that war now exists against the ethical decay common to so much of the unbelieving world. If we are not to block the continuing blessings of God upon our life, firm action is necessary!

> Put to death, therefore, whatever belongs to your earthly nature: sexual immorality, impurity, lust, evil desires and greed, which is idolatry. Because of these, the wrath of God is coming. You used to walk in these ways, in the life you once lived. But now you must rid yourselves of all such things as these: anger, rage, malice, slander and filthy language from your lips. Do not lie to each other, since you have taken off your old self with its practices and have put on the new self, which is being renewed in knowledge in the image of its Creator. (Col. 3:5-10)

The Colossian heresy

Here is a list of *character virtues* – utterly different from the ritualistic demands made upon the followers of the incipient Gnosticism that so threatened the infant church at Colosse.

Bible students have called this the Colossian heresy. Its leaders called for their followers to follow certain external abstinences and to live like super-spiritual hermits, in the belief that the way to the deeper life lay there. We recognise them by their fussy rules: *Do not handle! Do not taste! Do not touch!* (Col. 2:16-21).

This is the approach of a number of non-Christian belief systems today, in their call for certain procedures that will guarantee a richer, fuller spirituality. The demands are for ritual washings, strict dietary requirements; rules affecting headdress and clothing, postures and gestures.... 'but', as Paul says, 'they lack any value in restraining sensual indulgence' (Col. 2:23).

Our great aim – what is it? During a conference, I was interviewing John Stott, and I asked him 'What are you looking forward to more than anything else?' He replied, 'I think I can honestly say that, more than anything, I look forward to being more like Jesus Christ.'

More of Christ

And this was the aim of the apostle Paul: 'But one thing I do: Forgetting what is behind and straining towards what is ahead, I press on towards the goal to win the prize for which God has called me heavenwards in Christ Jesus' (Phil. 3:13, 14).

'The prize'.... what could that have been? The answer lies throughout the entire letter to the Philippians – for the name of Jesus occurs on average every two verses. The prize is this: *More of Christ in my life.*

Nothing, then, must be allowed to block such a blessing. Yet almost anything can become a block. Money, sex and power can do it. Take money. In John Bunyan's *The Pilgrim's Progress*, the travellers – Christian and Hopeful – come to a little hill called Lucre, close to a silver mine:

Then I saw in my dream, that a little off the road, over against the silver mine, stood Demas (gentleman-like), to call to passengers to come and see; who said to Christian and his fellow, 'Ho, turn aside hither, and I will show you a thing.' Christian: 'What thing so deserving as to turn us out of the way?'

And that is the issue. Almost anything can deflect a servant of Christ from the way of knowing Him and having Him at centre point. It is all too possible that the smallest personal quirk – even to the very Christian work that we are involved in – can subtly move into the place reserved for Him alone.

We are never going to wake up one morning and murmur, 'My goodness, I do believe that I've become holy.' But hold on to two lines from John Whittaker's hymn, *Immortal Love for ever full*:

'To turn aside from Thee is hell,
To walk with Thee is heaven.'

19

Sifting Through Spirituality

'Spirituality' is a popular way by which many describe their personal viewpoint today. They may not attend any place of religious worship, but nevertheless have embraced a certain feel for transcendency in their outlook on life. This was apparent at the time of the death of Princess Diana in 1997. The thousands of flowers, candles and shrines placed outside Buckingham Palace were expressing a wistful belief that something existed outside the steel-and-concrete life of the West. I commented on this in an article I was invited to write for a national newspaper at the time:

> .... Diana's death had profoundly touched four basic human needs; *first* there was guilt and our fundamental need to atone for the wrong that we do. Prompted by their guilt in relation to Diana, many were looking into other areas of their personal lives at that time, and conducting an audit of their behaviour.... *Secondly*, there was the primaeval need to unite in the face of danger and sorrow.... *Third*, there was the desire in so many people around the world to make their mark, the need to go somewhere and do something which showed that we cared. This is what all

those flowers and the queues to sign books of condolence were about…. *Finally*, her untimely death brought to the surface the fundamental need in all of us to survive…. (*The Express*, Sunday, 30 August 1998)

These instincts, and more, give us our cue for sensitive witness, for they all lie deep down in the human psyche.

For all true *Christian* spirituality flows directly from a dramatic weekend in the Middle East 2,000 years ago; two events – the death and resurrection of Jesus Christ, with their two gifts, forgiveness and the Holy Spirit; calling for two responses – repentance and faith. The early preaching in the Acts of the Apostles is full of it.

What feeds us?

'Spirituality' is a buzzword today. At its heart it deals with the question, *What makes you tick, and grow as a Christian? Where is your epicentre? What feeds and animates you?* If we were looking for a Scripture passage that deals with the progress and spiritual growth of believers, we might opt for Paul's letter to the Colossians. There, the basic framework for the believer's experience is taken up and is contrasted with the false philosophies and pseudo-spiritualities of the time. Here are pointers to 'the new self' that is being renewed in the image of the Creator; it outlines the Christian qualities that can be expected in a growing believer; readers are to let the word of Christ dwell in us, as we meet at the Lord's Table, as we teach and admonish one another, and as we sing psalms and spiritual songs, doing everything in the name of the Lord Jesus.

What then builds us in knowing the true and only God? How can we become more like His Son, Jesus Christ? What makes for growth in moral character and develops us as a true disciple? Here are several components:

THE INHERITED BACKGROUND

Think of the hymns that many of us grew up on. Think of Timothy's faith that first lived in his grandmother and mother (2 Tim. 1:5). There was the hymn writer John Newton who – on the high seas – never forgot his mother who had taught him to pray before she died, when he was eight.

So often it is the women who have been key. Libanius, the fourth-century teacher of rhetoric, exclaimed: 'What women these Christians have!' Among his students was John Chrysostom, the golden-mouthed preacher of Constantinople, whose mother, Anthusa, was the behind-the-scenes secret of his upbringing. The inherited background.... all this speaks to us of *families*. Secondly:

THE LEARNT TRUTHS

My own diet as a child was Bible stories, with which the Scriptures teem. There was story after story after story. As I grew up, my own worldview was imperceptibly developing, with the four mighty planks of *Creation*, our human *Fall*, that of *Redemption* and the final *Triumph* at Christ's Return.

Let daily Bible reading be a personal daily *delight*! Jeremiah declared, 'When your words came, I ate them; they were my joy and my heart's delight.' David the Psalmist knew this. 'I rise before dawn and cry for help. I have put my hope in your word.' That sounds like a habit! Isaiah knew this too. 'The sovereign Lord has given me an instructed tongue, to know *the word* that sustains the weary. He wakens me morning by morning, wakens my ear to listen like one being taught.' Regular Bible reading and personal prayer ought to be like the meeting of lovers for an agreed appointment.

In time, there should become formed in our minds mighty truths that undergird our entire outlook on life – Faith....

Grace…. Forgiveness…. Justification…. Judgment. *Our task, as we teach our families, groups and whole fellowships, is to prevent a childlike church from becoming a childish church.* Thirdly:

The Mission Imperative

All convinced believers should want to share what they have been freely given by grace, on a one-to-one basis. But there is preaching too; preaching that demands a verdict. To quote Richard Baxter, of Kidderminster, parish in the seventeenth century:

> I preached, as never sure to preach again,
> and as a dying man to dying men.

But the mission takes the two forms of what John Stott once called *the verbal* and *the visible.* These two emphases certainly characterised the Anglican group in London, that became nicknamed *The Clapham Sect,* two centuries ago. Their activities touched the whole world and culminated in the momentous abolition of the slave trade in 1807.

From their efforts – and their successors – came the forming of the Church Missionary Society, the British and Foreign Bible Society, the Church Pastoral Aid Society, the London Missionary Society, and a cascade of other works of evangelism, social reform and practical mercy.

Ashley Cooper

A successor to the Clapham group was Ashley Cooper, the seventh Earl of Shaftesbury, renowned for his enduring work for the poor and deprived, and the reforming Acts that he ensured were passed in Parliament on behalf of the children in the collieries and factories. If you have a hat, you should take it off as you walk up London's Shaftesbury Avenue and into Piccadilly Circus, for there at the very heart of the capital is a visual reminder of gospel witness, in the statue of Eros that was put up to commemorate a man who combined the verbal and the visible in such a rich degree.

This is an up-and-doing spirituality. Certainly, the Scriptures are paramount; Wesley prayed that, as a preacher, he would be 'homo unius libri' – a man of one book. Yet there was other urgent work to be done! The London celebrity Dr Samuel Johnson once complained, 'I hate to meet John Wesley. The dog enchants you with his conversation, and then breaks away to go and visit some old woman.'

Christian experience seems to indicate that a thorough-going biblically based spirituality results in a massive release of energy. When we read of Hannah More, of London's *Blue Stocking Club* – friend of the Clapham Sect – and of what were termed her 'cheap repository tracts' that flooded England at the rate of two million a year (and this in a population of only nine million); when we learn of her revolutionary approach to Sunday Schools and to schooling in general among the deprived people of Somerset, we can only wonder at the sheer impact of the gospel of grace upon a single life.

The vision of a few

Today, there are camps, houseparties, beach missions and student fellowships. They found their origin not in a committee decision, but through the vision of a tiny few. My mother was the first-ever treasurer of the world Inter-Varsity Fellowship that began at Cambridge University. She had no chequebook, and kept no accounts. The entire finances she kept in a biscuit tin under her bed at Girton College.

It seems that God takes an individual; a Gideon, a Deborah, a Timothy or a Wilberforce or a Joni Eareckson Tada, and says, 'Get together with a few others, and see what you can do.'

The motivation for all mission is nothing less than the glory of God. We are to see ourselves as a royal priesthood, declaring the praises of Him who called us out of darkness into his wonderful light. It follows, then, that when we are reaching out to declare the things of Christ to others, we are actually doing the priestly job; we are doing spirituality! Here is a fourth aspect:

THE ENDURED HARDSHIPS

I find myself puzzled at the frequent absence of this component in a number of published descriptions of spirituality. For the inclusion of hardship and suffering is built into Christian spirituality. We follow a Man who Himself suffered. We also are to recognise that God has chosen the path of suffering for our own spiritual progress and depth of discipleship. The seventeenth-century Puritan minister, Stephen Charnock, once preached on Psalm 10, verse 1 – 'Why, O LORD, do you stand far off? Why do you hide yourself in times of trouble?' Charnock had this to say about 'trouble':

> Without it we shall be as light as a weather-cock, moved with every blast of evil tidings; our hopes will swim or sink according to the news we hear.

A vital question is, 'Are the truths we hold to of such importance that we are prepared to suffer, even to die for them?' C.H. Spurgeon, preaching on 1 Corinthians 9:25, asked 'If we will not take pains for the kingdom of heaven, what kingdom will we take pains for?'

Hardship as a Christian, then, is one of the earliest themes that we need to teach to those newest in the faith. More will follow on this topic in chapter 22.

The word Hapax

Here, then, are four basic components of a biblical spirituality. Other elements might have been mentioned. The Lord's

Supper is rightly valued across the world as a meeting that draws lovers close to their Lord, and to one another. But we end this chapter by suggesting that a Christ-based spirituality can be summed up by a single word in the Greek of the New Testament. It is the word *Hapax* – *'once'*…. *'once for all.'* We find it in Jude 3: 'I felt I had to write and urge you to contend for the faith that was **once for all** entrusted to the saints.' We also will find the word in such passages as Hebrews 7, verse 27: 'He (Christ) sacrificed for their sins once for all when he offered himself.'

There is nothing to be added

From the occurrence of *hapax*, we learn that what God has *said* – in the faith once delivered to the saints – He has said once for all. There is nothing more to add, *though **we** have plenty more to learn!* And we learn from the Hebrews passages that what God has *done*, in the saving death of His Son, He has done once for all. Nothing is to be added to this redemption; it cannot be repeated, nor is it to be overlaid with ordinances or traditions that obscure or compromise the complete finality of Christ's sacrifice for our sins.

It is to what God has said, once for all, and to what God has done once for all, that we are to be witnesses, in our personal discipline, and in our guardianship and proclamation of Christ's good news to a dying world. *Hapax*…. our epicentre ultimately can be described by that single word!

20

Sustaining
the Long-Term

When I was sixteen, my parents gave me a copy of the Greek New Testament. In the flyleaf, they had written the Greek text of 2 Timothy 2:3: 'Endure hardship as a good soldier of Jesus Christ' (NKJV). Then at the age of twenty-two – on entering theological college – I received a pocket Bible from Mr Nash, who had first steered me into Christian discipleship. There, in the flyleaf, was written the same text. No one could say I had not been warned....

Massive encouragement is given in the golden chapter of Isaiah 40, where the prophet declares that though youths would grow weary, and young men would stumble and fall, 'they that wait upon the LORD shall renew their strength; they shall mount up with **wings as eagles**; they shall **run,** and not be weary; and they shall **walk**, and not faint' (Isa. 40:31, KJV).

But then, why the seeming diminishing of tempo, as the great chapter ends? Why not close with *Walking.... Running.... yea, FLYING!* But Isaiah has it in the reverse order. Perhaps the reason is that – although running can be exciting, and flying even thrilling – it is *walking* that is more important in the long-term. The apostle John indeed contrasts 'walking' in truth and obedience with the teacher who **'runs ahead and does not continue in the teaching of Christ'** (2 John 4, 6, 9).

On entering a new phase of Christian activity, plenty of us make most of our mistakes in the first six months, and have brazenly attempted to hit the road running, if not flying! But how does the servant of God stay intact ten, twenty, fifty years down that road? Generally, it is to be the steady *walk* for us, undertaken from the start in a spirit of humility, and with certain resolves predominating. Here are some of them:

STAY SERVANT

It is those who wait 'upon the LORD' who will renew their strength for the task ahead. It was this that enabled leaders such as Isaiah, Daniel or the apostle Paul to outface the harshest regimes of world dictators in their own time.

Take Paul alone! Basketed over the Damascus wall, rejected at Antioch, threatened in Iconium, stoned at Lystra, frustrated in Bithynia, flogged in Philippi, hounded in Thessalonica, ridiculed in Athens, harassed in Ephesus, arrested in Jerusalem, tried in Caesarea, shipwrecked at Malta, imprisoned in Rome. What held Paul, when man after man deserted him and let him down? *Why, it was the fact that he was an apostle;* he had been sent by none other than Jesus Christ! 'Servanthood' underlay everything he touched, whether among his jailers, the Gentiles, the seafarers or the politicians.

It is servanthood that holds us for the long-term. Servanthood bears the sense of accountability – to the One who died for me upon the Cross, *and therefore to others for whom He also died.* We have said earlier that the saints of God do not take long to recognise whether this quality is present or not in their leader. Once it is proved, then virtually anything is possible!

Shepherds who feed themselves

Jude has only condemnation for those who soar like dazzling rockets into the ecclesiastical firmament – widely hailed for a period, but still 'shepherds who feed only themselves.... clouds without rain, blown along by the wind; autumn trees without fruit.... wandering stars' (Jude 12, 13). They were never servants, and by the end they will be out of view.

Stay servant! This does not mean that service for God makes me a doormat. Jesus was the Servant of all; yet authority was stamped upon everything that He did. The Cross of Calvary exhibited this double-sided dimension supremely, and it is therefore a daily closeness to Calvary that bestows this unique blessing upon all true gospel undertakings.

STAY STUDENT

'They that hope/wait.... upon the Lord'. Here is the lesson of the appetite. If it is the Lord Himself who governs all that we do – His Person, His rule, His Word – then we shall stay learners for ever. We can never plumb the depths of all that there is to know of Him, and the Scriptures will prove to be an inexhaustible reservoir, whatever age we reach.

Taking notes

Billy Graham was sixty-nine when, one Sunday evening in London, he decided to attend All Souls Church with his wife Ruth. David Turner, the lay reader, was the preacher that evening, and was somewhat anxious that the Bible passage that night was 'Now concerning the Unmarried' – barely a suitable topic for a travelling grandfather! David need not have worried. *Mr Graham had his Bible open, and sat taking notes throughout the sermon.* When he ran out of paper, he nudged his wife for more. Three days later, he asked for the recording of the sermon. Six weeks later – from California – we were asked whether there were any more recordings from the series that we might send to Mr Graham.

It was a lesson for us all. There are some spiritual practitioners who reach their ceiling by their mid-twenties. It seems that they have no more to learn. Their public speaking never improves at all; they seem incapable of listening, or taking advice from anybody. Their service has stopped still in its tracks.

The regular prayer should be, *Let me stay student; make me hungry!* When the leader stays hungry, the fellowship stays hungry.

STAY VIGILANT

'Waiting upon the Lord....' Surely this attentiveness has been characteristic of every faithful servant of God. The Lord told Ezekiel, 'Son of man, I have made you *a watchman* for the house of Israel.' Habakkuk declared, 'I will stand *at my watch* and station myself on the ramparts.' 'But as for me,' cried Micah, '*I watch in hope for the LORD, I wait for God my Saviour.*' '*Watch out,*' said Jesus, 'that no one deceives you.' Paul wrote, 'Let us not be like others, who are asleep, but *let us be alert* and self-controlled.' '*Watch out,*' warns John, 'that you do not lose what you have worked for.'

It is for oneself, for one's family, for fellow believers, for society at large and for kingdom openings and opportunities, that the eyes of our perception are to be kept open – permanently! Such wakefulness on our part can only develop, first, through *regular attention to Scripture.* Cumulatively, over the years, we begin to gain something of the mind of Christ Himself.

The liberal death wish

When we read Paul's letters, it is the necessary awareness of error that surfaces time and again. This has to be a part of our own vigilant service. The journalist Malcolm Muggeridge once commented on what he called 'The Great Liberal Death Wish' in church circles:

> It is indeed among Christians themselves that the final assault on Christianity has been mounted. All they had to show was that when Jesus said his kingdom was not of this world he meant that it was. Then, moving on from there, to stand all the other basic Christian propositions similarly on their heads (*Conversion*, Collins, p. 63).

How then to stay clear – whether from doctrinal deviation or indeed moral lapse? Sometimes church leaders fall into disgrace and are obliged to resign from public responsibility. This seems to occur, often because there has not been enough vigilance, either *by* them, or *for* them; such tend to have been 'loners', with little close fellowship and insufficient accountability.... to spouse and family, and to the watchfulness of colleagues. Although space must be provided for necessary privacy, it is still important that answers can be given to the question as to where we are and whom we are with, at any given time.

Further, it is steady intercessory prayer for others that maintains vigilance for those under our pastoral oversight. In our prayer list, we will come across a name and the thought arises, *What's happening? I've not seen them for a while? I must find out.*

Vigilance is required on a number of fronts. But now what of this, for a fourth requirement of staying on the long road?

STAY VALIANT

Unless they *did* 'wait upon the Lord', courage and resilience would inevitably evaporate from Isaiah's readers and – in the face of the overwhelming odds that faced them – they would indeed 'faint'. In this life, we can never be far from the power displays of the kingdom of darkness. Boldness, in service for God, is more than a matter of frantically uttering slogans; it is an entire outlook on life that recognises the church as being at the very centre of God's interests! The church is not a sideline of the Lord undertaken as a part-time activity while attending to the greater affairs of the world's nations, and indeed the universe. *The church that Jesus Christ died for is what God is all about!*

That being so, no wonder those early apostolic believers were so buoyant. Told unequivocally to stop preaching in Christ's name, they turn to prayer (Acts 4:18-31) – NOT to ask that the authorities relent, or be removed, but that they, Christ's followers, be given yet *more* boldness to preach!

Astride smoking Babylon

Ours is the vision of Christ and His church at the centre of all things, finally to be seen standing astride the grave of smoking Babylon (Rev. 19:1-3). This enables us to pray, plan, work and proclaim with every expectation of victory, whatever the setbacks. Christian speakers should confidently stand – Bible open – before a collection of people, thinking inwardly, *In the next few minutes, somebody's life is going to be changed.*

True, downright opposition may confront us, as it did Bunyan, who spent twelve years in prison because of his open-air preaching. The Puritan Richard Baxter endured a similar fate. It has happened before, and the signs are that it will happen again, here in the West, as it is indeed taking place in numerous parts of the world at present.

Some of us will become buffeted across the passage of time, but Jesus taught us to expect nothing else (John 16:33). Others will know extreme weakness, as did that intrepid missionary, Amy Carmichael of Dohnavur. Serving the Lord for fifty-five years in India, she touched thousands for God, while nevertheless enduring considerable pain and illness. A poem of hers spells out the issue:

> Hast thou no scar?
> No hidden scar on foot or side, or hand?
> I hear thee sung as mighty in the land;
> I hear them hail thy bright ascendant star,
> Hast thou no scar?
>
> Hast thou no wound?
> Yet I was wounded by the archers, spent;
> Laid me beside a tree to die – and rent
> By ravening wolves that compassed me.
> I swooned; hast thou no wound?
>
> No wound, no scar?
> Yet as the Master, shall the servant be,
> And pierced are the feet that follow Me;
> But thine are whole.
> Can he have travelled far,
> who hath no wound, no scar?

It is those people – the Amy Carmichaels of this world – who show us how long-term ministry is done and maintained. *Ultimately, it is the sense of calling that keeps us on the road.* It was this sense that kept Wesley on track. The last letter he ever wrote was on 24 February 24 1791. It was addressed to William Wilberforce – then in the direst throes of his campaign against slavery:

> Unless God has raised you up for this very thing you will be worn out by the opposition of men and devils; but if God is with you who can be against you? O be not weary in well-doing. Go on, in the name of God and in the power of his might, till even American slavery, the vilest that ever saw the sun, shall vanish away before it.

The letter was sent. Six days later at the age of eighty-eight, the great evangelist was gone, having shown us, like Isaiah, how long-term ministry is maintained – until Heaven takes over.

Part Five:

When the Heat Turns On

Today's world has reached a stage which, if it had been described to preceding centuries, would have called forth the cry, 'This is the Apocalypse!'

ALEKSANDR SOLZHENITSYN
Templeton Award Address, London, 1983

21

The Worldwide
Challenge of Evil

I once adapted the words of Psalm 46, so that they could be sung to the inspiring tune of *The Dambusters March*, and many are the times when I have heard the hymn sung. However, another side to the famous World War II bombing of Germany's Mohne Dam was put to me when, after church one day, I was introduced to a saintly German worshipper who had actually been a resident of the Mohne Valley the night that *617* Squadron had dropped its bombs.

'It was the most terrible night of our lives,' she confided. 'As the dam crumbled, we knew what was about to happen. 'I survived, but very little did. And then the noise! Almost worst of all was the anguished cries of the thousands of animals around us.'

It was the prophet Isaiah who was inspired to use the sombre flood image to describe what his people would be facing, on returning to their Jewish homeland at the end of their exile under the Babylonians. There would be challenges ahead, marauders on every side, and the very powers of Satan himself ranged against God's people. But they would be supported by the Lord of Hosts!

When the enemy shall come in like a flood, the Spirit of the
Lord shall lift up a standard against him. (Isa. 59:19, KJV)

Our evil adversaries

The modern Bible commentator Alec Motyer makes a convincing case for the King James Version as being better than the modern versions at this point. The word translated 'enemy' in the King James Version, he says, is the same Hebrew word as in verse 18 just before, where the sentence is very clearly referring to *the evil adversaries of God*. The older reading is preferable: *When the enemy shall come in like a flood, the Spirit of the Lord shall lift up a standard against him.'*

Against *what?* 'Against HIM' is the phrase. It seems to be personal. We must put on one side the shallow theories that regard evil as something caused by circumstances, and therefore something that circumstances can eventually put right. Traditional communists used to believe in a perfectible Utopian ideal, a workers' paradise – achievable here on earth. *They were always going to be disillusioned.*

Learn to stand back

Christians do not think like this. We have never believed that evil can be dealt with by rearranging society's furniture. We are actually faced by 'an enemy'. *And Isaiah's is the big view.* We must learn, as he did, to stand back a little from the close-range view of evil's impressionistic picture, thrust before us by every twist of the media. As we daily wait on God and His Word, we can obtain the wider picture of His kingdom – His overarching rule and work in all our restless human affairs…. and see the end from the beginning.

If we can do that, then we can live with the ongoing tensions, and even learn to cope when – as Isaiah puts it – the enemy seems to come in like a flood… threatening, terrifying and unprincipled, like the Assyrians of old, in his own time, and the terrifying empires that would follow after.

All of this points to an even bigger picture still, because Isaiah is pointing on beyond Judah of eighth century B.C.; he is looking *telescopically* to the coming of Jesus and the restoration and salvation, that He would bring, in the gospel. Even more than that, Isaiah transports us into the far reaches of eternity – to the future glory of the new heaven and the new earth, when the earth shall be filled with the glory of God as the waters cover the sea.

King, Servant, Conqueror

If we, as Christ's followers, can see that, we will not only *survive* when the enemy comes in like a flood, but we will triumph – for the God we trust in is King; He is Servant; and He is Conqueror.

True, even in this part of the prophecy – following God's restoration of His people – there certainly is an enemy to be reckoned with. The divine, conquering Warrior enters the scene, and He doesn't like what He sees! He sees *'that there was no one, he was appalled that there was no one to intervene'* (v. 16). Thus we read on: 'His own arm worked salvation for Him.' Verse 17 describes the Lord arming Himself for the conflict with evil.

The implication is that God does it all; He is the great protagonist and fighter … but He chooses to involve us! He looks for even that one person who, in a given situation, will be found standing there in the breach, when the dam – that has been holding back evil – gives way…. and great swirling waters are released upon the earth.

The waters of persecution

There is an enemy, coming in at times like a flood. God's people are all too aware of the waters of persecution and martyrdom – more in the last 100 years than in all the other centuries put together; the boiling whirlpools of ethnic, tribal, racial and cultural divides that engulf whole countries; the swirling currents of sectarian error and speculation gone mad.

When error and evil are rampaging on the loose, the temptation is, mentally and spiritually, to give up.

The enemy is so strong, it seems… and he is a person. He comes to Adam and Eve in the garden with beguiling talk, and they cave in; rebellion and sin enter into our situation and this enemy, a fallen and rebelling angel, brings other angels down with him; and the human race, in its own fallenness becomes part of this scene of worldwide rebellion against the Creator. We are part of it all.

We should take heart that evil was not present from eternity. God and goodness have always existed. If evil was eternally coexistent with God, then the French writer Baudelaire might have been right when he said, 'If there is a God, he is the devil.'

Evil represents a Departure

But no. Genesis chapters 1–3 – and the rest of the Bible – cut off that blasphemous argument. Evil does not originate in eternity, and doesn't come from God at all. It represents a departure rather than a first cause. As Augustine, sixteen centuries ago, commented, *'The evil angels, though created good, became evil by their voluntary defection from the good, so that the cause of evil is not the good, but defection from the good'* (*City of God*, Book 12).

And we were made, not as robots, *but as moral beings*, with the capacity to choose and love and obey. If we argue that we should not have been created that way, we are asking that the human race should not exist at all, and that creation should have been halted after the formation of plants and animals. No, we were made for a relationship of love and worship.

But then the Fall was followed by God's great rescue act – demonstrated supremely in the dying love and sacrifice of Jesus Christ, and the gift of His Spirit in the lives of His people. All will end in the final triumph of goodness over evil, and the eternal rule of God in Christ. The whole apparatus of evil will be dismantled for ever.

We are not, then, to fall into what is called 'dualistic' thinking – belief in two *equal and eternal systems* operating side by side, the good and the bad. Evil is not eternal, and nor is Satan. Who, then, is the opposite of the Devil? It is not God, or

Jesus. They are eternal. The opposite of Satan is *another* angel; the angel *Michael*, the great conqueror of Satan in the battle that took place *spiritually* while the earthly event and victory of the Cross was happening outside Jerusalem. We read of that spiritual conflict in Revelation 12, where Satan was defeated by Michael, and the Cross of Jesus was the reason.

The thrashing death throes of Evil

The Devil and his empire, though overcome at the Cross, are not finally destroyed – yet! Don't complain! For if all evil were wiped out at a stroke now, what are the chances that you might be wiped out with it? *We are still given time to take sides.* The empire of evil is in its thrashing death throes, according to Revelation 12, verse 12: 'The devil has come down to you in great wrath, knowing that his time is short' (RSV).

We stay encouraged. Christ's army is working and witnessing not towards victory, but *from* victory already achieved. Thus, when enraged by his impending destruction, the enemy comes in like a flood, it is with great confidence that we gather and fight.... under *the standard* that the Spirit of the Lord shall lift up!

What is this 'standard'? Isaiah himself gives us the answer in an earlier chapter. About the distant future, he writes:

> In that day the Root of Jesse will stand as a banner for the peoples; the nations will rally to Him, and His place of rest will be glorious.... He will raise a banner for the nations and gather the exiles of Israel; He will assemble the scattered people of Judah from the four quarters of the earth. (Isa. 11:10, 12)

Now it becomes clear. Jesse was the father of King David; and thus the head of David's line. The 'root' of Jesse points to *Jesus*, the ancestor of the ancestors. Jesus stands so big in Scripture that He is both the root (the origin) *and* 'the offspring' of David, the son of Jesse. In Revelation 22, verse 16, the glorified Jesus says, 'I am the Root and the

Offspring of David, and the bright Morning Star.' One of the old hymns describes Jesus as *'Great David's Greater Son'*.

The Banner is Jesus

Jesus Himself is the standard, lifted up by the Spirit of the Lord, when the enemy comes in like a flood. It is around Him that we gather in our mission to a dying world.

First, a standard is a symbol of **Battle**. As the old hymn puts it, *'The Son of God rides out to war, the ancient foe to slay. His blood-red banner streams afar – Who follows Him today?'* It is the Christ that **died** who is the symbol and standard before us in the battle with sin and evil.

Second, a standard is a symbol of **Unity**. *Soldiers* gather around a standard. *Combatants* – aware of how weak they are on their own – will flock to a standard that they love and recognise. In John 12, verse 32, Jesus was referring to the Cross when He said, 'I, when I am *lifted up* from the earth, will draw all men to myself.' Our once-crucified Leader is able to draw under His banner of love men and women, boys and girls, from every nation on earth.

Third, a standard is a symbol of **Conquest**. Originally, the Cross must have looked like a symbol of defeat. But no longer. By this standard that He represents, we read that Christ 'disarmed the principalities and powers, making a public example of them' (Col. 2:15, RSV). Under such a banner, we have joined the winning side.

Fourthly, a standard is a symbol of **Direction**. *'Forward March,'* is what it is saying. If we come under the banner that is a Person, we can be sure that we are part of a kingdom that is advancing and will outlive all others.

We are not to become too daunted in the face of today's evils. Rather, we should search our own hearts, lest *we* have pockets of evil that we are accommodating.

Make it one of your memory verses! Isaiah 59:19; 'When the enemy shall come in like a flood, the Spirit of the Lord shall lift up a standard against him'(KJV).

22

For the Name

'So what did you say to all the ministers under your care?'
I was sitting at lunch with a prominent church leader,
during the great Global Anglican Future Conference in
Jerusalem. His leadership was under threat in a country
where the church authorities above him were insisting that
he not diverge from a particular doctrine that they held as
vital.

Was it the doctrine of the Cross that they were insisting on ? The truth of Justification by Faith? The deity of
Jesus? Far from it. It was a newly introduced piece of revi-
sionist teaching that undermined one of the great Creation
laws of the Bible:

> For this reason a man will leave his father and mother
> and be united to his wife, and they will become one flesh.
> (Gen. 2:24)

This fundamental law on marriage was endorsed by Jesus,
when he quoted from the Genesis passage (Matt. 19:3-5).

I listened for my friend's reply.

'Half of my colleagues were encouraging me, under this pressure, to lead them all in seceding from the church to which we belonged, and begin afresh under a new loyalty. The other half were begging me not to depart – thus leaving them in the hands of revisionists who were denying the authority and name of Jesus.

'So I said to them all, "We are in the middle of a great storm. But Jesus is with us in the boat. If we can keep our eyes upon Jesus, He will show us what to do. But if we have our eyes on the storm itself, it will destroy us."'

As I write this page, my friend is still in place. But for how long?

The War on Christians

This is but one common form of modern persecution against the name of Christ. *It comes from within.* In other parts of the world, the pressure is from without, when it is punishable by death to hold to Christ's Name in the face of the beliefs insisted on – frequently by state-backed militant groups. In a major *Newsweek* article entitled 'The War on Christians', Ayaan Hirsi Ali reported that since 2003 terrorist attacks on Christians in Africa, the Middle East and Asia had increased by 309 per cent (*Newsweek*, 12 February 2012).

Essentially, it is the authority and Name of Christ that has been the offence throughout history. From the earliest days, Jesus warned His followers for all time:

If the world hates you, keep in mind that it hated me first. If you belonged to the world, it would love you as its own. As it is, you do not belong to the world, but I have chosen you out of the world. That is why the world hates you. Remember the words I spoke to you: 'No servant is greater than his master.' If they persecuted me, they will persecute you also. If they obeyed my teaching, they will

obey yours also. They will treat you this way because of
my name, for they do not know the One who sent me.
(John 15:18-21)

The implication of these words is that – outside of Christ
– God cannot be known at all. Jesus so completely mirrors
the nature of God the Father, that anyone who turns away
from Jesus has lost the opportunity of knowing God.

Salvation in no one else

There is, then, mighty power in the name of Jesus. In the
book of Acts, chapter 4 and verse 12, the apostle Peter declared to the religious leaders in Jerusalem, *'Neither is there
salvation in any other: for there is none other name under heaven
given among men, whereby we must be saved.'* (KJV) How the
apostles were hated, because of their preaching of this
Name! *The Name of Jesus....* Its power acts as a magnet,
for – depending on the polarity of the metals brought into
contact with it – one will be immediately attracted, but another violently repelled.

Earlier in John chapter 15, the theme of spiritual intimacy with Jesus is the emphasis. 'I have called you friends,'
He says. But now, from verse 18, another side is put, namely,
the hostility to Christ's Name that the family of Jesus will
be required to face.

In John 15, we read of love, but also of hate. Here is our
first recognizable contrast in Jesus' teaching:

LOVE AND HATE

If we left off reading at John 15: 17, we would have an unbalanced view of Christian discipleship. Love – yes! As I write,
Christ's love has drawn over 2.3 billion people under His banner worldwide. But love is not the full story. The Christian
way of life is indeed a love story, but it is also a hate story:

If the world hates you, keep in mind that it hated me first.
If you belonged to the world, it would love you as its own.
As it is, you do not belong to the world, but I have chosen
you out of the world. That is why the world hates you....
He who hates me hates my Father as well. (vv. 18, 19, 23)

The world – the society that has organised itself against
the rule of God – is mentioned five times in these few sentences. The German Christian leader Dietrich Bonhoeffer,
whose defiance of the Hitler regime led to his own death
at a concentration camp in 1945, wrote prophetically, *'The
messengers of Jesus will be hated to the end of time. They will
be blamed for all the divisions which rend cities and homes. Jesus
and His disciples will be condemned on all sides for undermining
family life and for leading the nation astray. They will be called
crazy fanatics and disturbers of the peace.'*

The contrast here in John 15 is between love and hatred.
There is a second:

SELECTION AND REJECTION

The breathtaking truth of Selection is there earlier in John
15, where Jesus told His followers 'You did not choose me,
but I chose *you*' (v. 16).

I was once privileged to interview Joni Eareckson Tada,
whose witness as a quadriplegic from a wheelchair has
touched millions of people around the world. My final question to her was, 'And what has been the greatest surprise of
your life? She replied, 'Oh, that's easy to answer. My greatest surprise is that Jesus should have chosen *me* – following
my diving accident at the age of seventeen – to know Him,
and then even to be used by Him among so many.'

This wonderful truth of Selection by Christ is there
in (v. 19), but it runs hand in hand with the experience of
Rejection by the world.

When rejection becomes visible

Naturally, in a country with a long legacy of Christianity, the gulf between Selection and Rejection may not always be starkly apparent. As the Baptist preacher Alexander Maclaren once commented, 'A half-Christianised world and a half-secularised church get on well together.' But let the weather deteriorate, the climate of opinion harden – and the flimsy veneer will disappear. It doesn't take much to make the world's rejection of us become visible.

There was a mighty gospel worker years ago called Kate Booth; she was the eldest daughter of General Booth of the Salvation Army. She took her team of 'Hallelujah Lasses' to Europe. In France – witnessing in the dives and brothels of Paris – she was so brave that she was dubbed by a military name, 'La Maréchale.' In Switzerland, her vigorous street preaching caused such opposition that she was put into prison. My parents heard her when she was an old lady, and they said she was electric. Kate was uncompromising. When in her twenties, she once declared:

> Jesus was crucified. Ever since that day, men have tried to find an easier way, but the easier ways fail….Things have changed, you say; there is liberty now. Is there? Go and live Christ's life, speak as He spoke, teach what He taught; denounce sin wherever you find it, and see if the enemy will not turn on you with all the fury of hell. *(The Heavenly Witch*, Carolyn Scott, Hamish Hamilton, p.113)

It is the Name of Christ that draws the dividing line. There seems to be a third contrast we can draw from the Lord's teaching:

POWER AND PERSECUTION

The power of prayer – and fruit-bearing – among Christ's followers is present in the first half of John 15. 'Ask what you will,' said Jesus, 'and it will be given you' (v. 7). Our part is to bring our requests to Him in His Name, with His Word and with His interests at heart.... and we leave the rest with Him, *knowing that we were heard, and answered.*

There is also the blessing of fruit-bearing (vv. 8, 16). We take this to mean growth in the fruit of the Spirit in life and character, together with effectiveness in service and the winning of others to Christ's side – the side of Jesus. There is power there!

But as we move on, we read of persecution. 'Remember the words I spoke to you: No servant is greater than his master. If they persecuted me, they will persecute you also' (v. 20).

The Name and all it stands for

It is a biblical pattern: Power is the promise – for prayer, for Christian growth, for effective living and the overcoming of temptation – but the Name, and all that it stands for, is too threatening for the unbelieving world to accommodate. Even in the face of Christ's work and His miracles, people would still cling to the sins and habits of a lifetime. They would have only themselves to blame; that is the sense of Jesus' allusion to Psalm 35, when he said: 'They hated me without a cause.'

To ignore Christ's healing power for the soul is to be left without excuse. Growing up as I did on the lower slopes of Mount Kenya, there were no doctors or hospitals nearby. When, one night, a dire illness struck a number of our African neighbours, all my missionary father could do was to leap into his car and travel many miles to obtain the right counteracting drug from a doctor. The doctor refused to come himself; he simply handed my father the drugs, swabs and some injection needles, and told him to get on with it.

It was all extremely hard work. My Dad got back and some thirty people accepted the injection. All of them recovered. However, there was one man who refused the treatment, and disappeared back to his home; he was never seen alive again.

Once apply this to the Bible scene and we can recognise that, on a spiritual level, God had sent His agents of cure for the Jewish nation; messengers, judges and prophets – but repeatedly the cure was refused. 'They hated me without a cause' was eventually fulfilled in Christ.

Why continue on?

Some might ask, 'Why, in the face of these adversities, do we put up with the cost of going on? Why continue at all? The late Hassan Dequani Tafti, of Iran, himself a convert to Christ, put it very clearly once: *'Is it not an amazing thing'*, he asked, *'that such a clear-cut and stern demand should be made by someone in history, and that, nearly 2,000 years after, it should still carry with it a power to attract people?'*

And we would agree in wonder ourselves, with the many thousands who today are accepting Christ in countries of active persecution – despite the harassment and killing of so many of them. Why is 'Counting the Cost' apparently scarcely an issue with them?

Even here, it is Christ who Himself gives the answer, when in verses 26 onwards, He speaks of the Counsellor, the Holy Spirit, who comes to every believer, bringing into life and personality His own very presence, and assuring His follower, even at the point of execution, 'You have been with ME from the beginning' (vv. 26, 27). *The magnetism lies there. It is worth martyrdom.*

Across the centuries there has been an ongoing magnetism in serving the One who bears the Name that is above every Name.

23

Wrestling in Prayer

It seems that Abraham wrestled in prayer for the wicked city of Sodom (Gen. 18); Moses wrestled for his people in the wilderness (Num. 11). The apostle Paul wrestled for the Christians of Corinth, and writes of Epaphras who was always 'wrestling in prayer' for his friends in Colosse (Col. 4:12).

What is this 'wrestling'? The term in the Greek New Testament is that used by secular writers for the 'wrestling' that was common in the Greek games of the time. The object of such wrestling was the pinning down of one's opponent *and keeping him in an unyielding hold*. And that is what wrestling in prayer means . This is clearly not the pattern of everyday prayer, but rather that of a specific prayer of limited duration, inspired for the targeting of a particular crisis.

The wrestling that will not let go
This 'wrestling' is best understood as the exercising of a firm 'hold' *that simply will not let go*. That is the wonder of prayer. Only get in the flow of the prayer fellowship that now straddles the world – and we can learn within an hour of some tragedy or outrage affecting fellow believers on a distant

continent. *By this kind of targeted prayer, we can be as effectively by the side of our hurting friends as if we were there in person.*

A missionary example

Out in Kenya, my parents were once in a severe crisis about the car that was vital to them as missionaries, in the pioneer work that was theirs. Their ancient, battered Ford V8 box body had broken down in a dusty town known then as Fort Hall, and £20 was the price quoted for its repair – a handsome sum in the early 1940s. But they were completely destitute of cash. They knelt by the car and prayed….

Dad then looked in at Fort Hall's dusty post office. A single letter was waiting for him. It had been sent from a friend in England, weeks earlier. It read, *'We have been praying very much for you today, and God seems to have laid it specifically on our hearts that you are going to need a particular sum of money. What it is to be used for, only you will know. Please accept this sum of £20.'*

This was an example of *targeted* prayer, exercised from many days back, and many thousands of miles away.

It is a way of life for us; to learn how to target a sudden crisis involving a family or a work of God, in the interests of Christ and His kingdom. But let us follow some biblical examples of prayer that wrestles:

WRESTLING – IN GOD'S WORK

One example may be taken from the mid-fifth century B.C. – of Nehemiah, a child of the Jewish captivity in Babylon. The exile was now officially over; the first exiles had already returned from Babylon nearly a hundred years earlier; yet Judah was still under the overall rule of Persia.

Prayer is independent of distance

It was around 445 B.C. that some of the former exiles came back to Nehemiah – still in the Persian city of Susa

– telling of the 'great trouble' and continuing 'disgrace' of Jerusalem's broken walls and burnt gates (Neh. 1:2, 3). The news broke Nehemiah's heart. A crisis? To him it certainly was, even though, having been born during the exile of God's people, he had never actually seen Jerusalem. But the City of David represented his spiritual home. Weepingly, he began to pray. *And prayer of this kind brings heaven and earth together.* As butler to King Artaxerxes in the palace at Susa, Nehemiah was far from Jerusalem. But his heart reached out five hundred miles away. His burning desire was to leave his work in the palace, travel to Jerusalem and begin the work of restoration.

Prayer reduces every giant

But how was permission to be obtained from the most powerful man in the Middle East? We learn, from the close of Nehemiah's heartfelt words, how targeted prayer cuts even the mightiest down to size. 'Give your servant success today by granting him favour in the presence of *this man*' (Neh. 1:11). Prayer of this kind reduces the size of the giants that confront us – removing the panoply and emblems of power – for in the sight of the Lord of history, no political or religious tyrant can ever be more than 'this man'.

Prayer can obliterate time

'Give your servant success **today**,' had been the prayer of the butler who was eventually to become governor of Judah. Yet the heartfelt request – uttered in November-December, the month of 'Kislev' (Neh. 1:1) – was not granted until *four months later*, in the month of Nisan (Neh. 2:1-9).

What, then, was the God of heaven *doing* in the four months between Nehemiah's prayer and the breakthrough moment at the royal dining table? The answer is given, in the words of Jesus, centuries later: 'My Father is always

at his work to this very day, and I, too, am working'
(John 5:17). *God never stops working*; the times are in His
hands; He is just as concerned and active five minutes
before the breakthrough takes place, as He is five minutes
afterwards.

And no mighty potentate or dictator ever escaped the
verdict of Proverbs 21:1, 'The king's heart is in the hand
of the LORD; he directs it like a watercourse wherever he
pleases.'

Now however, we can move to a further example of
wrestling prayer, from words written by the apostle Paul:

WRESTLING – IN GOD'S VICTORY
In his letter to the Christians at Ephesus, Paul was conclud-
ing with a reminder of what the church is up against, in all
its work and witness:

> Finally, my brethren, be strong in the Lord, and in the
> power of his might. Put on the whole armour of God, that
> ye may be able to stand against the wiles of the devil. For
> we wrestle not against flesh and blood, but against princi-
> palities, against powers, against the rulers of the darkness
> of this world, against spiritual wickedness in high places.
> Wherefore take unto you the whole armour of God, that
> ye may be able to withstand in the evil day, and having
> done all, to stand. (Eph. 6:10-13, KJV)

It was only after a French member of our church became
naturalised as a Briton that we smilingly reminded each
other of one big difference that changing nationalities
meant. 'Before I changed over,' she said, 'The Battle of
Waterloo was a defeat. Now it's a victory!'

We have entered the winning side
It does not take long for new disciples of Jesus Christ to
sense something of the same. They had been under the

power of the world, the flesh and the devil, and had never realised it. Now, however, with the Cross coming into view, they have entered upon the winning side.

But the powers of evil do not readily admit defeat. 'The devil has come down to you in great wrath', writes the apostle John, 'because he knows that his time is short!' (Rev. 12:12, RSV). Satan is like a powerful dictator who, in a brief conflict with an invader, is out of the capital and has lost his centre. *His next stop is the border.* It was the Cross of Calvary that ensured his defeat. The resurrection of Christ was the headline that proclaimed it. The next stop is the return of Christ. After that, the lake of fire (Rev. 20:10).

Meanwhile, he struts, boasts and threatens. Believers, however – living in the power of Christ – have the authority, in the words of the old English Prayer Book, to 'beat down Satan under our feet'. The devil has limited power only to tempt, and no more. If we give way to his seductions, it is only because we choose to do so. Our responsibility, then, is to strengthen our motivation and our resolves with a daily renewing of our vision of *Christ*, so that the desire to stay winning is maintained.

The pieces of armour

The apostle Paul would have been chained to a Roman guard when he wrote his letter to Ephesus. No doubt his reference to the different pieces of armour would have been inspired by the sight of the breastplate, the shield and the helmet…. and by the sight of the sword, which he equates with the Word of God. *And there was wrestling involved.* This is where prayer came in.

Indeed, there are occasions involving overt evil when, covering ourselves under the protective power of Christ and His blood, we must pray deliberately *against* 'the wiles of the devil,' and – without letting go – claim the sure victory of the Cross, where Christ disarmed the principalities and powers (Col. 2:15). There are four main areas of occult activity; **Superstition**, plain and simple; **Fortune-Telling** in some thirty different forms (including use of rod and pendulum and card reading); **Magic** in about eighteen forms (including healing or 'white' magic); and **Spiritism** in some thirty forms (including table lifting, glass moving, automatic writing and seances). But, against the claimed victory of the Cross, these powers have no option but to retreat.

Young believers are wise to leave direct ministry against such powers to those authorised and more experienced within the church. Some unfortunately develop a taste for such work; others can become so unbalanced that – instead of recognising the three-fold enmity of the world, the flesh and the Devil – tend to place every problem under the last category.

But wrestling at certain times, and in the certain victory of God, comes the way of many. It should happen more often in the grim realities of our world today. There is a third kind of wrestling. We see it in Jacob:

WRESTLING – IN GOD'S PRESENCE

Genesis chapter 32 brings God's fearful, unreliable and restless patriarch Jacob to a night in his travels when a Man wrestles with him until daybreak. Despite his action to desist, by wrenching Jacob's hip joint, *Jacob will not let go*. It is the hymn writer Charles Wesley who, in his mighty hymn 'Come, O thou Traveller Unknown,' identifies the Man as the pre-incarnate Second Person of the Trinity, for as Jacob declares afterwards, 'I saw God face to face, and yet my life was spared' (Gen. 32:30). As Wesley phrases it in verse 3:

In vain Thou strugglest to get free, I never will unloose my hold!

Art Thou the Man that died for me? The secret of Thy love unfold;

Wrestling I will not let Thee go, Till I Thy Name Thy nature know.

Here in prayer is an encounter with the living God; yet we know from John 1:18 that no man can see God and live. This, then, has to be the same pre-incarnate Jesus who, in the book of Daniel, was seen by the terrified Nebuchadnezzar to be accompanying Shadrach, Meshach and Abednego in Babylon's fiery furnace (Dan. 3:25). Such 'Jesus appearances' occur frequently in the Old Testament.

The lessons we learn from Jacob's experience, as he seeks more of the Lord's blessing in his life, are several. First, *it can be too easy to let go early!* Indeed, one's mind can cease to be occupied on the main object, and begin to drift: 'I must answer that email…. What's for dinner tonight?'

We can also be *content to settle for too little.* Some 'blessings' we can too easily put back on the shelf. After all, this was the pre-incarnate Christ that Jacob was dealing with! What would He *not* give him?

Our godly ancestors would often keep a prayer diary, and write down the specific requests that they had wrestled over in prayer – and would monitor the answers that could later be written down, complete with dates. If Jacob had done this, he would have been able, by Genesis 35, to write, I'm no longer to be called Jacob. God has renamed me **Israel** – *'He struggles with God.'*

This is the wrestling that will not let go!

24

Connecting with the Final Day

It was just on midnight as the new millennium began, when fireworks burst over Sydney's Harbour Bridge, and the word **Eternity** was then revealed in neon lights a hundred feet high. It was Australia's tribute to Arthur Stace, who – decades earlier – as an illiterate alcoholic, had accepted Christ. From then on, as an anonymous chalk artist, he would script the word *Eternity* in chalk, on walls and pavements, as many as fifty times in a single night. Not for thirty years was his identity known. Eventually Arthur became known as 'Mr Eternity'.

Eternity – and how we live in the light of the approaching Final Day – confronts every servant of Jesus Christ:

> Then I looked, and there before me was the Lamb, standing on Mount Zion, and with him, 144,000 who had his name and the Father's name written on their foreheads. And I heard a sound from heaven like the roar of rushing waters and like a loud peal of thunder. (Rev. 14:1, 2)

A 'LOOK' AT MOUNT ZION AND THE FOLLOWERS OF THE LAMB (REV. 14:1-5)
If, on reading this page, you have been a follower of Christ for just *two days*, you have the names of Christ and the Father

written invisibly and irreversibly on your forehead, and you are among the 144,000! The 144,000 are not an elitist group, for they are redeemed 'from the earth,' and were purchased 'from among men' – that is, from humanity in general (vv. 3, 4). Although Revelation 7:9 reveals that those in heaven will be *a great multitude that no one could number,* 144,000 – as a multiple of twelve (Israel's twelve tribes of the Old Testament and the twelve apostles of the New Testament) – is a symbolic number for all God's people.

'Mount Zion' symbolises God's heavenly dwelling (Isa. 35:10; Heb. 12:22). Thus, as John Calvin asserted 450 years ago, *'heaven is where Jesus is.'*

The emphasis of the New Testament is not on *our departure* so much as on *Christ's Return.* **On the Last Day, Christ will be bringing heaven and the new Jerusalem *with* Him,** and God Himself will be dwelling with us (Rev. 21:3). What makes heaven *'Heaven'* is Jesus. Just to be with *Him!* Sometimes critics ask us caustically whether people like themselves will get to heaven. Our reply must be, 'The very centre of heaven itself is taken up with Jesus. All eyes will be on Him! Would you *wish* to be with Jesus for all eternity? Would that be heaven for you, or hell?'

Rehearse the life of heaven

The difference between heaven and hell is Jesus. Even in this life, heaven itself can be rehearsed. The prisoners in Philippi's jail would hear Paul and Silas singing in the next cell; their jail had become a chapel (Acts 16:25). In 1636, the Scottish preacher, Samuel Rutherford, was arrest for his beliefs. But, writing from his place of banished isolation, he would write his address: *Christ's Palace, Aberdeen.*

In verse 3, John writes of the 'new song' of the 144,000, only learnt by the redeemed. For *that* song we must wait for heaven itself, but meanwhile we can *rehearse* with our worship below. Aim for the best and omit the tiringly repetitive and forgettable! It was Søren Kierkegaard, who – outraged by the poor standards of his time – wrote scathingly that 'Even to worship God is to subject him to ludicrous twaddle' *(Attack on Christendom,* 1854*).*

In character building, too, emulate the 144,000! Their undefilement with women (v. 4) speaks of their refusal to compromise their fidelity to Christ. Paul uses similar language of the church's marriage to Christ alone (2 Cor. 11:2).

Those on Mount Zion, in their purity, loyalty and dignity, are selected as God's choicest 'firstfruits'. 'No lie was found in their mouths' – for by the time they reach heaven they are found 'blameless', as *firstfruits* heading a mighty procession into the new order!

But the second paragraph presents a darker vision:

A LOOK AT BABYLON AND THE FOLLOWERS OF THE BEAST (REV. 14: 6-13)
Here we have the first of three angels, giving warning of the particular aspect of the gospel that speaks of *judgment.* For what results when we slam the door on the creative, saving love of God in Jesus Christ? The answer is that we have chosen our own way, in self-banishment. And hell is but the divine underlining of our decision *that we don't want Christ.* The issue is there in verse 7: who or what are we going to worship?

The first of these messages of approaching judgment is phrased **universally**; it is addressed *'to every nation, tribe, language and people'* (v. 6). From the second angel (v. 8) the judgment is addressed **prophetically** – against the throne of evil, symbolised by wicked Babylon, whose downfall is so certain as to be reported as a past event (v. 8).

The third angel (v. 9) speaks of the coming judgment **terminally,** this time upon the worshippers of 'the beast' –

that across history represents the apparatus of anti-Christian politics combined with false religion (Rev. 13). The language is of both *the wine of God's fury* and of *burning sulphur.*

Visitors to the site of ancient Sodom and Gomorrah, on which 'the Lord rained down burning sulphur' (Gen. 19; compare Jude 7), will not see a tree or blade of grass for square mile after square mile of salt and desolate destruction.... and this is only *one* image used to describe the final end of the beast and those who follow him (v. 10).

Whether it is in terms of fire, outer darkness, a cup of fury or everlasting destruction, all these are vivid descriptions of a *reality* – separation from God for ever – and they are enough to make any servant of Jesus weep, pray, work and preach. *For Jesus, by His Cross of love, has already drunk of that bitter cup on their behalf, if they will but accept it.* The contrasts apparent here are enough to drive us to our knees:

A sobering contrast

For example, the Lamb's followers have a new song; the Beast's followers (v. 11) have no rest. The Lamb's followers are sealed for eternity, with God's name on their foreheads; the Beast's followers (v. 9) are branded with his mark. The Lamb's followers are secure, 'purchased from among men' by God Himself; the Beast's followers are lined up with fallen Babylon. The Lamb's followers, by the power of the Cross, are pure and blameless; the Beast's followers are tainted with Babylon's adulteries. The Lamb's followers follow Him, and – through death – are *'blessed'* (v. 13); the Beast's followers drink a cup of wrath (v. 10). The Lamb's followers (v. 13) are wonderfully promised that *their deeds will follow them....* in those they had won to Christ, the children they had taught, the witness they had maintained, their resistance against the world, the flesh and the devil, their prayers, their love, their service.... nothing will be lost; *their deeds will follow them!* But for the Beast's followers, only rising smoke will be the final result of their achievements.

All.... 'this', we read (v. 12), 'calls for *patient endurance* on the part of the saints who obey God's commandments and remain faithful to Jesus.'

In the final paragraph of our passage, we are reminded once again of the centrality of Jesus.

A LOOK AT THE HARVEST, AND THE REAPING OF THE EARTH (REV. 14:14-20)

Travelling on the bumpy roads of Tanzania one day, my driver pulled up beside a roadside worker who was busy trimming the dusty border.

'Thank you!' called out my companion; 'Thanks for the great job you're doing!'

'Ah well,' smiled the African. 'I'm doing this because the President's on his way!'

Here in Revelation 14, on this infinitely greater and universal scale, we are warned that the returning Son of Man *is on His way*. It is the next item on the agenda... and we are to be prepared. An angel calls to the seated world Master, 'Take your sickle, and reap, ... for the harvest of this earth is ripe' (v. 15). We may wonder how a created angel can seem to be directing orders to the crowned King of heaven. But the clue is that the angel had come directly 'out of the *temple*' (v. 15); the message to reap having been issued from God Himself.

There is a noticeable difference in the language here. *The harvest* (vv. 15, 16) is a phrase used indeed by Jesus: 'Ask the Lord of the harvest, therefore, to send out workers into his harvest field' (Matt. 9:38). The implication is that Christ's wielding of the *harvest* sickle refers chiefly to the gathering in of His own people, to be with Him for ever.

The Harvest Home or the Great Winepress

By contrast are words *from the angel of judgment*, addressed to his fellow angel, 'Take your sharp sickle and gather the clusters of grapes from the earth's vine, because its grapes are ripe' (v. 18). The destination of this 'harvest' was *the great winepress of God's wrath* (v. 19). There is a difference between being gathered into the harvest home of Christ, or consigned to the winepress of divine wrath.

Naturally, our critics can only think of divine wrath in human terms – as vindictive, malicious and irrational. And such were the gods of Greek mythology, with their little jealous love affairs and spiteful rivalries. In contrast to that is divine wrath in its purity; the steady, unwavering antagonism of Goodness against Evil; standing against all that would defy the Lord in the blaze of His eternal holiness.

It is, unfortunately, a shallow view of salvation that we find in some outreach programmes today, when the Lord is spoken of almost as a kind of Best Pal that 'we need'. True, we do need Him, but the deeper truth is that – as rebels from the beginning – we are an *offence* to the Creator; the sentence of judgment upon us has been passed; we are already under His wrath. Commenting on the words 'We were by nature children of wrath' (Eph. 2:3, KJV), the former Anglican teacher, Handley Moule, described the shallow view I have referred to as:

> .... 'other Gospels, which are *not* another'.... They present (man) rather as an unfortunate traveller upon some bye-road of the universe, fallen among thieves, 'more sinned *against* than sinning', cruelly robbed and maimed, with

nothing to blame but his enemies and his circumstances; so that the supreme King stands in some sense obliged to redress him, and to recover him, and to comfort him after his long calamities.

The sin within the sinner

Many are the times it has been said, 'God hates the sin, but loves the sinner.' It is well meant, but it is a shallow statement. The biblical truth stands that *it is simply not possible to separate the sin from the sinner* – as though our problem was somehow the fault of sin, or of Satan! Sin is not some different entity outside of us; it is within, *the great sin* being the shutting out of Christ and His salvation from our lives. This being so, we dare not minimise what men and women bring upon themselves in the earth's final reaping.

Our pastoral application to all this? Chiefly it lies in the quality of a life of Spirit-filled witness to a dying world, as we follow the most perfect Being who ever walked. Sixteen centuries ago, John Chrysostom, of Constantinople, said that just as a beautiful coat only looks its best when worn on a body, so the Scriptures – even though wonderful when proclaimed in public – are far more stupendous when they are being lived out by the people who hear them!

When that is happening, Jesus has, to a wonderful degree, become visible, tangible, attractive and accessible – and then comes the possibility of a world revival!

25

Standing in the Gap

In 1865, an American author, Mary Mapes Dodge, wrote the story of the brave fifteen year-old Dutch boy, Hans Brinker, who – by plugging his finger into a leaking dyke throughout a stormy night – was able to save the precarious landscape of Holland from the incoming, cascading seas.

Here we take up the theme of heaven's servants who have played a key part by standing in the gap, when the walls of righteousness in a nation are being breached. How to prevent the pouring in of evil? How to avert the judgments of God from flooding upon a land? Yet, across history godly men and woman have played a humble part by standing in the gap when no messengers could be found.

One such messenger was Ezekiel, living with his fellow Jewish exiles in the baking heat and swamps of Babylonia, five hundred miles from his home in Jerusalem. God – he declared – was on a vain search for the right *intercessor*, to stand in the gaps of society's walls, and so protect people from approaching disaster and divine judgment:

> The people of the land practise extortion and commit rob-
> bery; they oppress the poor and needy and ill-treat the alien,
> denying them justice. I looked for a man among them who
> would build up the wall and stand before me in the gap on
> behalf of the land so that I would not have to destroy it, but
> I found none. (Ezek. 22:29, 30)

The question might well have been asked, 'In this situation
of exile, was there a point in *bothering* any further, when
God's blessing was so manifestly absent from Jewish society
just then?'

The voice of prophecy

Some would feel that way about life in the West at the present
time when – despite numerous and extremely exciting points
of growth – the general public view is that, since the end of
World War II, the voice of prophecy has moved away from
the church to the theatre. Meanwhile, with virtually every
piece of legislation passed by largely unbelieving politicians,
the institutions are tending to push the church out into exile
– and there, at most, to *contain* it.

It is only those standing in the gap of our civilisation's
precarious walls who realise that if Christianity were taken
out of our society – together with its Christian Sunday, the
rock of marriage, its freedom of worship, its care of the
sick and dying, its ethics, its toddlers' groups, pensioners'
clubs, youth camps and the like – our inherited civilisation
would disappear as well, with all its privileges…. *and yet
society would never realise why it had become so unhappy.*

> 'When the foundations are being destroyed,' wrote David
> the psalmist, 'what can the righteous do?' (Ps. 11:3).

Closing the aperture

The answer seems to be, Let *someone* with faith, humility
and courage step forward willingly, into the breach. *Ezekiel*

and his exiled friends had lost everything, out there by the river Chebar. Yet this was the substance of the divine message: 'I looked for a man among them' – *anyone* – 'who would build up the wall.' So great is the mercy of God that He looks for a person, someone whose interceding presence closes the aperture.... but we read, 'I found none.'

Interceding servants of the Lord stand in the gap, facing two ways; towards the world, on behalf of God, and towards God on behalf of the world. It is possible to express the basic elements of this calling by various vivid biblical symbols. Take Isaiah, then:

THE BURNING COAL – AND GOD'S CLEANSING

Isaiah was confronted by the same problem that faced Ezekiel: *'And (God) saw that there was no man, and wondered that there was no intercessor'* (Isa. 59:16, KJV).

From the very start, a sense of utter unworthiness and sin overwhelmed the young Isaiah who would have been about the same age as the legendary Hans Brinker. Faced by the commissioning vision of the enthroned Lord, he cried, *"Woe to me! I am ruined! For I am a man of unclean lips, and I live among a people of unclean lips, and my eyes have seen the King, the Lord Almighty"* (Isa. 6:5). The New Testament identifies the glowing personage of Isaiah's vision as none other than the pre-incarnate second Person of the Trinity. For John's Gospel quotes from Isaiah 6 with this statement, 'Isaiah said this because he saw *Jesus'* glory and spoke about *him*' (John 12:41).

Reassurance to the young prophet comes through a divine symbol; the live coal – which usually features in the context of the wrath of God; His inaccessible holiness and the blazing purity of His law and covenant. But the fact that the live coal is taken from the *altar* reassures Isaiah, for the altar was the place where the divine wrath was propitiated by the shedding of blood. The angelic seraph makes the interpretation plain: 'See, this has touched your lips; your guilt is taken away and your sin atoned for' (Isa. 6:7).

A brand plucked from the burning

Every genuine calling by the Lord for service must be marked by such an assurance before true and valid service can be given. John Wesley could only humbly call himself 'a brand plucked from the burning'. The mission of God starts with our own forgiveness, and continues with the *daily* cleansing that we need, symbolised by that live coal taken from the very altar of God. It is those witnesses for God, whose every day begins with the remembrance of Calvary, who are likely to have access to the very heart of their listeners.

For Isaiah, that was the start of a ministry that outlived four monarchs and has inspired Bible readers across the world. But we move from Isaiah to Moses – and a further biblical emblem of calling:

THE HALLOWED STAFF – AND GOD'S AUTHORITY

Here is presented the strange combination of the weak and the majestic. Moses has his own experience of the fire of God, in the encounter of the burning bush (Exod. 3:1-10), but then comes the moment when his credentials must be established! Moses had been a 'Somebody' in the court of Pharaoh, but he is now in a foreign land, engaged in casual labour. He was aware of no great skills, but the Lord says to him, 'What is that in your hand?' (Exod. 4:2).

Moses looks down. *It's a stick.* What's more absurd than a stick from the desert? Yet by that stick, Pharaoh's magicians would be confounded, the natural life of Egypt would be disrupted, waters would be parted, rocks split – and a whole nation set on the move.

Moses the eloquent

But the staff was nothing by itself. Moses, for his part, is completely inept as a speaker – he has to get Aaron to speak for him. Yet by the time we arrive at the famous utterances of Deuteronomy 32, he has quite evidently become one of the most eloquent of all preachers that ever lived. Moses is the perfect example, not of a born speaker but of a *made* speaker, who stood in the gap on behalf of his people:

> So (God) said he would destroy them – had not Moses, his chosen one, stood in the breach before him to keep his wrath from destroying them. (Ps. 106:23)

Moses' stick has inspired humble workers for the Lord across the ages. 'What is that in your hand?' It may not be much! That feeble, absurd stick stands for disappointing academic records, lack of funds, few natural aptitudes, social disadvantages and an apathetic people around us. *What of it?* God seems to have chosen the absurd, the foolish things of this world, to confound the wise – and weak human instruments who nevertheless ministered in the authority of God.

From the hallowed staff, we move on:

THE PROPHETIC MANTLE – AND GOD'S SPIRIT

Now to Elijah! There is an *edge* to the mission of God, for true service for Him will compel a verdict. This was so in that bulldozer of a preacher, the prophet Elijah. In the crossing of the Jordan's waters (2 Kings 2:8), we have a re-run of Moses and the parting of the water, but here it is the mantle of Elijah that occasions the miracle. Elijah's successor-to-be, Elisha, is about to assume the mantle of his mentor.

There appears the chariot of fire, and Elijah is whirled to glory. Elisha sees the discarded mantle on the ground *and he takes it over.* The message is not lost on the prophets standing by. 'The *Spirit* of Elijah', they observed, 'is resting on Elisha' (2 Kings 2:15).

Passing the mantle

The wonder of Christian service is that the same 'mantle' of spiritual power becomes passed down the generations. 'Can such a mantle be bequeathed to me?' we might ask. In answer, my wife Pam would instance the example of a single woman, born in the 1920s, called Maud Hall. Pam, when aged ten, 'went forward' in response to Christ, following a Saturday-night gospel service in Allerford Chapel in south London. Maud was her 'counsellor'; short, with hair in an old-fashioned braid above her head, no make-up and 'with a sweet and very holy face'. *Maud stood in the gap* for person after person, during her lifelong service of Jesus Christ. Besides her numerous other contacts around London, she maintained contact with Pam for years afterwards, with regular prayer and frequent letters.

There could not have been a greater contrast between the fiery Elijah and Maud Hall! *Yet both were possessed by the same Spirit.*

God's calling is to those who will stand in the gap on behalf of others. From Isaiah, Moses and Elijah, we come to the apostle John:

THE COMMISSIONING SCROLL – AND GOD'S CALL
The emphasis of this biblical emblem can be summed up by the phrase 'the bitter and the sweet'.

> Then the voice that I had heard from heaven spoke to me once more: 'Go, take the scroll that lies open in the hand of the angel who is standing on the sea and on the land.' So I went to the angel and asked him to give me the little scroll. He said to me, 'Take it and eat it. It will turn

your stomach sour, but in your mouth it will be as sweet as honey'. (Rev. 10:8, 9)

In this vision from the book of Revelation, the apostle John takes the little scroll and devours it.... and indeed experiences the promised bitter-sweet sensation. This 'scroll' – held out by a mighty angel (vv. 1, 2) – seems to represent a *recommissioning* of God's servant in a reassuring interlude between the awesome sixth and seventh trumpets. John is then told, 'You must prophesy again about many peoples, nations, languages and kings' (v. 11). Centuries earlier, Ezekiel had received a similar vision, he himself being commissioned to 'speak to the house of Israel' (Ezek. 3:1).

Never 'our' message

The reason for the *eating* of the scroll is that the words are never to be those of the messengers; they are to be put into their mouths by the *Lord*. We are only mandated to pass on to others what has been given from God's Word.

And the bitter-sweet tang – *this is the inevitable experience of anyone who ever stood in the gap for Jesus Christ.* There is nothing sweeter, nothing more satisfying, than being in the very work of God. But *there is the pain aspect to it as well.* The reason is obvious; the Leader we serve was Himself rejected and killed, and we must learn what it means to walk in His steps. Surely anyone who has faithfully stood in the gap has known adversity.

So is the whole thing worth it? All depends upon whose call it is. When that diminutive missionary to the Chinese, Gladys Aylward, died during the night after a lifetime of standing in the gap that opened before her, they found in the morning some words in the flyleaf of the Bible by her bed:

God won't ask you for certificates,
He'll only ask if you've been faithful to your call.

A Prayer of Blessing for Each Other

We servants of the Lord commend one another in mutual affection and trust to the love and safe keeping of God our *Father*. May He ever make His way plain before our face, and lead us along the high road of His eternal purpose.

May our *Lord Jesus Christ* give us the good cheer of His presence and the strength of His leadership day by day.

May the *Holy Spirit* fill us with love, wisdom and power – to commend the gospel of salvation both by our life and our teaching.

May the *Lord* lead us where we go, and keep us when we sleep, and talk with us when we wake; and may His peace which passes understanding, and His love which is beyond all knowledge guide, guard and prosper us, now and evermore. Amen.

Christian Focus Publications

Our mission statement –

STAYING FAITHFUL

In dependence upon God we seek to impact the world through literature faithful to His infallible Word, the Bible. Our aim is to ensure that the Lord Jesus Christ is presented as the only hope to obtain forgiveness of sin, live a useful life and look forward to heaven with Him.

Our Books are published in four imprints:

CHRISTIAN
FOCUS

popular works including biographies, commentaries, basic doctrine and Christian living.

CHRISTIAN
HERITAGE

books representing some of the best material from the rich heritage of the church.

MENTOR

books written at a level suitable for Bible College and seminary students, pastors, and other serious readers. The imprint includes commentaries, doctrinal studies, examination of current issues and church history.

CF4·K

children's books for quality Bible teaching and for all age groups: Sunday school curriculum, puzzle and activity books; personal and family devotional titles, biographies and inspirational stories – because you are never too young to know Jesus!

Christian Focus Publications Ltd,
Geanies House, Fearn, Ross-shire,
IV20 1TW, Scotland, United Kingdom.
www.christianfocus.com
blog.christianfocus.com